Measuring Up

to the

Ohio Academic Content Standards

and Success Strategies for the Ohio Achievement Test

Reading

800-822-1080
www.OHStandardsHelp.com

PEOPLES®
PUBLISHING GROUP
299 Market Street, Saddle Brook, NJ 07663

D0840195

Publisher: Diane Miller
Editorial Development: e2 Publishing Services
Vice President and Editorial Director: Marie Spano
Vice President of Marketing: Victoria Ameer Kiely
Director of Marketing: Melissa Dubno Geller
Vice President, Production and Manufacturing: Doreen Smith
Pre-Press & Production Manager: Jason Grasso
Editor: Scott Caffrey
Project Manager: Christina Grupico
Production Editors: Christina Grupico
Copy Editors: Josh Gillenson, Michele Wells
Proofreader: Dee Josephson
Permissions Manager: Kristine Liebman
Photo Researchers: Pat Smith, Robert E. Lee
Cover Designers: Cynthia Mackowicz, Michele Sakow
Illustrators: Armando Báez, Dan Lish, Sharon MacGregor,
Anni Matsick, Ed Tadiello

Ohio Advisory Panel:
Cherryl Mione, Hilliard City Schools
Betty Tanner, Language Arts Teacher

PEOPLES®
PUBLISHING GROUP

ISBN 1-4138-2159-6

Copyright © 2006
The Peoples Publishing Group, Inc.
299 Market Street
Saddle Brook, New Jersey 07663

Printed in the United States of America.

10 9 8 7 6 5 4 3 2

Measuring Up® Contents

Chapter 1 Word Analysis and Vocabulary Development 1

*Please see page (xiv) for an explanation of how Ohio Academic Content Standards are identified by letters and numbers in this Measuring Up® worktext.

Chapter 4 Informational, Technical, and Persuasive Texts 217

Correlation to the Ohio Academic Content Standards and Grade-Level Indicators

This worktext is customized to the Ohio Academic Content Standards and Grade-Level Indicators.
After the lesson is completed, place a ✓ to indicate Mastery or an X to indicate Review Needed.

Chapter 1: Word Analysis and Vocabulary Development

	Mastered Skill / Review Skill	1	2	3	4	5	6	7	8	IPT
Ohio Academic Content Standards Lessons										
(A) Acquisition of Vocabulary										
(A) Use context clues and text structures to determine the meaning of new vocabulary.		★	★	✓	✓	✓	✓	✓	✓	★
1 Define the meaning of unknown words by using context clues and the author's use of definition, restatement and example.		★	★	✓	✓	✓	✓	✓	✓	★
(B) Infer word meaning through identification and analysis of analogies and other word relationships.		★	✓	★	✓	✓	✓	✓	✓	★
2 Use context clues to determine the meaning of synonyms, antonyms, homophones, homonyms and homographs.		★	✓	★	✓	✓	✓	✓	✓	★
(C) Apply knowledge of connotation and denotation to learn the meanings of words.		★	✓	✓	★	✓	✓	✓	✓	★
3 Identify the connotation and denotation of new words.		★	✓	✓	★	✓	✓	✓	✓	★
(D) Use knowledge of symbols, acronyms, word origins and derivations to determine the meanings of unknown words.		★	✓	✓	✓	★	★	✓	✓	★
4 Identify and understand new uses of words and phrases in text, such as similes and metaphors.		★	✓	✓	✓	★	★	✓	✓	★
5 Use word origins to determine the meaning of unknown words and phrases.		★	✓	✓	✓	✓	★	✓	✓	★
7 Identify the meanings of abbreviations.		★	✓	✓	✓	✓	★	✓	✓	★
(E) Use knowledge of roots and affixes to determine the meanings of complex words.		★	✓	✓	✓	✓	✓	★	✓	★
6 Apply the knowledge of prefixes, suffixes and roots and their various inflections to analyze the meanings of words.		★	✓	✓	✓	✓	✓	★	✓	★
(F) Use multiple resources to enhance comprehension of vocabulary.		★	✓	✓	✓	✓	✓	✓	★	★
8 Determine the meanings and pronunciations of unknown words by using dictionaries, thesauruses, glossaries, technology and textual features, such as definitional footnotes or sidebars.		★	✓	✓	✓	✓	✓	✓	★	★

★ Grade-Level Indicator covered in this lesson

IPT—Independent Practice for the Test

✓ Grade-Level Indicator covered in past lessons

Correlation to the Ohio Academic Content Standards and Grade-Level Indicators

This worktext is customized to the Ohio Academic Content Standards and Grade-Level Indicators. After the lesson is completed, place a ✓ to indicate Mastery or an X to indicate Review Needed.

Chapter 2: The Reading Process and Comprehension

Ohio Academic Content Standards — Mastered Skill / Review Skill — Lessons	9	10	11	12	13	14	15	16	IPT
(B) Reading Process: Concepts of Print, Comprehension Strategies and Self-Monitoring Strategies									
(A) Determine a purpose for reading and use a range of reading comprehension strategies to better understand text.	★	★	✓	✓	✓	✓	✓	✓	★
1 Establish and adjust purposes for reading, including to find out, to understand, to interpret, to enjoy and to solve problems.	★	★	✓	✓	✓	✓	✓	✓	★
8 Monitor own comprehension by adjusting speed to fit the purpose, or by skimming, scanning, reading on, looking back or summarizing what has been read so far in text.	★	★	✓	✓	✓	✓	✓	✓	★
10 Use criteria to choose independent reading materials (e.g., personal interest, knowledge of authors and genres or recommendations from others).	★	★	✓	✓	✓	✓	✓	✓	★
11 Independently read books for various purposes (e.g., for enjoyment, for literary experience, to gain information or to perform a task).	★	★	✓	✓	✓	✓	✓	✓	★
(B) Apply effective reading comprehension strategies, including summarizing and making predictions and comparisons, using information in text, between text and across subject areas.	★	✓	★	★	★	★	✓	✓	★
2 Predict and support predictions with specific references to textual examples that may be in widely separated sections of text.	★	✓	★	✓	✓	✓	✓	✓	★
3 Make critical comparisons across texts.	★	✓	✓	★	✓	✓	✓	✓	★
4 Summarize the information in texts, recognizing that there may be several important ideas rather than just one main idea and identifying details that support each.	★	✓	✓	✓	★	✓	✓	✓	★
5 Make inferences based on implicit information in texts, and provide justifications for those inferences.	★	✓	✓	✓	✓	★	✓	✓	★
6 Select, create and use graphic organizers to interpret textual information.	★	✓	✓	✓	★	✓	✓	✓	★
(C) Make meaning through asking and responding to a variety of questions related to text.	★	✓	✓	✓	✓	✓	★	✓	★
7 Answer literal, inferential and evaluative questions to demonstrate comprehension of grade-appropriate print texts and electronic and visual media.	★	✓	✓	✓	✓	✓	★	✓	★
(D) Apply self-monitoring strategies to clarify confusion about text and to monitor comprehension.	★	✓	✓	✓	✓	✓	✓	★	★
6 Select, create and use graphic organizers to interpret textual information.	★	✓	✓	✓	✓	✓	✓	★	★
8 Monitor own comprehension by adjusting speed to fit the purpose, or by skimming, scanning, reading on, looking back or summarizing what has been read so far in text.	★	✓	✓	✓	✓	✓	✓	★	★
9 List questions and search for answers within the text to construct meaning.	★	✓	✓	✓	✓	✓	✓	★	★

★ Grade-Level Indicator covered in this lesson

✓ Grade-Level Indicator covered in past lessons

IPT—Independent Practice for the Test

This worktext is customized to the Ohio Academic Content Standards and Grade-Level Indicators. After the lesson is completed, place a ✓ to indicate Mastery or an X to indicate Review Needed.

Chapter 3: Literature

Ohio Academic Content Standards	Mastered Skill									
	Review Skill									
Lessons	17	18	19	20	21	22	23	24	25	IPT
(D) Reading Applications: Literary Text										
(A) Describe and analyze the elements of character development.	★	★	✓	✓	✓	✓	✓	✓	✓	★
1 Explain how a character's thoughts, words and actions reveal his or her motivations.	★	★	✓	✓	✓	✓	✓	✓	✓	★
(C) Identify the elements of plot and establish a connection between an element and a future event.	★	✓	★	✓	✓	✓	✓	✓	✓	★
3 Identify the main incidents of a plot sequence and explain how they influence future action.	★	✓	★	✓	✓	✓	✓	✓	✓	★
(B) Analyze the importance of setting.	★	✓	✓	★	✓	✓	✓	✓	✓	★
2 Explain the influence of setting on the selection.	★	✓	✓	★	✓	✓	✓	✓	✓	★
(D) Differentiate between the points of view in narrative text.	★	✓	✓	✓	★	✓	✓	✓	✓	★
4 Identify the speaker and explain how point of view affects the text.	★	✓	✓	✓	★	✓	✓	✓	✓	★
(E) Demonstrate comprehension by inferring themes patterns and symbols.	★	✓	✓	✓	✓	★	✓	✓	✓	★
5 Summarize stated and implied themes.	★	✓	✓	✓	✓	★	✓	✓	✓	★
(F) Identify similarities and differences of various literary forms and genres.	★	✓	✓	✓	✓	✓	★	✓	✓	★
6 Describe the defining characteristics of literary forms and genres, including poetry, drama, chapter books, biographies, fiction and nonfiction.	★	✓	✓	✓	✓	✓	★	✓	✓	★
(G) Explain how figurative language expresses ideas and conveys mood.	★	✓	✓	✓	✓	✓	✓	★	★	★
7 Interpret how an author's choice of words appeals to the senses and suggests mood.	★	✓	✓	✓	✓	✓	✓	★	✓	★
8 Identify and explain the use of figurative language in literary works, including idioms, similes, hyperboles, metaphors and personification.	★	✓	✓	✓	✓	✓	✓	✓	★	★

★ Grade-Level Indicator covered in this lesson
✓ Grade-Level Indicator covered in past lessons

IPT—Independent Practice for the Test

Correlation to the Ohio Academic Content Standards and Grade-Level Indicators

This worktext is customized to the Ohio Academic Content Standards and Grade-Level Indicators. After the lesson is completed, place a ✓ to indicate Mastery or an X to indicate Review Needed.

Chapter 4: Informational, Technical, and Persuasive Texts

Ohio Academic Content Standards	Lessons	26	27	28	29	30	31	32	33	34	35	IPT
(C) Reading Applications: Informational, Technical and Persuasive Text												
(A) Use text features and graphics to organize, analyze and draw inferences from content and to gain additional information.		★	★	★	★	✓	✓	✓	✓	✓	✓	★
1 Use text features, such as chapter titles, headings and subheadings; parts of books including the index and table of contents and online tools (search engines) to locate information.		★	★	✓	✓	✓	✓	✓	✓	✓	✓	★
5 Analyze information found in maps, charts, tables, graphs and diagrams.		★	✓	★	✓	✓	✓	✓	✓	✓	✓	★
6 Clarify steps in a set of instructions or procedures for proper sequencing and completeness and revise if necessary.		★	✓	✓	★	✓	✓	✓	✓	✓	✓	★
(B) Recognize the difference between cause and effect and fact and opinion to analyze text.		★	✓	✓	✓	★	★	✓	✓	✓	✓	★
2 Identify, distinguish between and explain examples of cause and effect in informational text.		★	✓	✓	✓	★	✓	✓	✓	✓	✓	★
7 Analyze the difference between fact and opinion.		★	✓	✓	✓	✓	★	✓	✓	✓	✓	★
(C) Explain how main ideas connect to each other in a variety of sources.		★	✓	✓	✓	✓	✓	★	✓	✓	✓	★
4 Summarize the main ideas and supporting details.		★	✓	✓	✓	✓	✓	★	✓	✓	✓	★
(F) Determine the extent to which a summary accurately reflects the main idea, critical details and underlying meaning of original text.		★	✓	✓	✓	✓	✓	★	✓	✓	★	★
3 Compare important details about a topic, using different sources of information, including books, magazines, newspapers and online resources.		★	✓	✓	✓	✓	✓	★	✓	✓	★	★
(E) Explain the treatment, scope and organization of ideas from different texts to draw conclusions about a topic.		★	✓	✓	✓	✓	✓	✓	★	✓	★	★
8 Distinguish relevant from irrelevant information in a text and identify possible points of confusion for the reader.		★	✓	✓	✓	✓	✓	✓	✓	✓	★	★
9 Identify and understand an author's purpose for writing, including to explain, to entertain or to inform.		★	✓	✓	✓	✓	✓	✓	★	✓	★	★
(D) Identify arguments and persuasive techniques used in informational text.		★	✓	✓	✓	✓	✓	✓	✓	★	✓	★
9 Identify and understand an author's purpose for writing, including to explain, to entertain or to inform.		★	✓	✓	✓	✓	✓	✓	✓	★	✓	★

★ Grade-Level Indicator covered in this lesson

✓ Grade-Level Indicator covered in past lessons

IPT—Independent Practice for the Test

to the
**Ohio Academic Content Standards
and Success Strategies for the
Ohio Achievement Test**

To the student:

How do you get better at anything you do? You practice! Just like with sports or other activities, the key to success in school is practice, practice, practice.

This book will help you review and practice reading strategies and skills. These are the strategies and skills you need to know to measure up on the *Ohio Achievement Test* for your grade. Practicing these skills and strategies now will help you do better in your work all year.

There are five chapters in this book. Chapter 1 helps you build your vocabulary and gives you practice analyzing different words. Chapter 2 takes you through the reading process and focuses on comprehension. Chapter 3 gives you practice reading literature. Chapter 4 gives you practice reading nonfiction.

This book gives you many chances to practice for the test. At the end of each chapter is an **Independent Practice for the Test** section. Each Independent Practice has a story for you to read. Following each story are multiple-choice questions and one short- or extended-response question that test your understanding. The stories and the questions are like the ones you may see on the actual test. Many of these questions are more difficult and will help you prepare for taking tests.

Next spring, you will take the *Ohio Achievement Test*. It will be an important step forward. Have a great year!

Measuring Up®

to the

**Ohio Academic Content Standards
and Success Strategies for the
Ohio Achievement Test**

To parents and families:

All students need reading skills to succeed. Ohio educators have created grade-appropriate standards called the Ohio Academic Content Standards for Reading. The standards describe what all Ohio students should know at each grade level. Students need to meet these standards, as measured by the *Ohio Achievement Test*, given in the spring. Students must learn to consider, analyze, interpret, and evaluate instead of just recalling simple facts.

Measuring Up® will help your child review the reading standards and prepare for all reading exams. It contains:

· lessons that focus on practicing the standards;

· varied reading selections;

· strategies and skills for reading independently;

· strategies and skills for answering testlike multiple-choice questions and short- and extended-response questions.

For success in school and the real world, your child needs good reading skills. Get involved! Your involvement is crucial to your child's success. Here are some suggestions:

· Read aloud to your child. Find a quiet place to read. If the book has pictures, talk about them. As your child listens, ask him or her to anticipate what will happen next. Talk about the characters and what happens to them.

· Treat reading as a pleasure, not a punishment. Give books as presents and show that you like to receive them, too. Respect each other's private reading time.

· Make sure your child has a library card. Visit the library together. Also visit bookstores. Attend author talks and storytelling sessions.

Work with us this year to ensure your child's success. Reading is essential not only for success in school but in the world as well. It will give pleasure throughout your child's life.

PEOPLES®
PUBLISHING GROUP

This book was created for Ohio students. Each lesson, question, and story will help you master the Ohio Academic Content Standards for Reading and do well on the *Ohio Achievement Test*. It will also help you do well on other reading exams you take during the school year.

About the Ohio Academic Content Standards

Ohio educators have set up standards for reading. They are called the Ohio Academic Content Standards. They spell out what all students at each grade level should know. Ohio educators have also created a statewide test for reading. It is called the *Ohio Achievement Test*. It shows how well students have mastered the Academic Content Standards. *Ohio Achievement Test* questions go along with the Academic Content Standards and meet the following objectives:

Reading Objectives

A. Acquisition of Vocabulary
B. Reading Process: Concepts of Print, Comprehension Strategies and Self-Monitoring Strategies
C. Reading Applications: Informational, Technical and Persuasive Text
D. Reading Applications: Literary Text

Format of the Ohio Achievement Test

The first part of the test contains vocabulary questions. Next, there are reading selections followed by questions. The reading selections are both informational and literary. You will be tested on three different types of questions—multiple choice, short answer, and extended response. Let's take a look at some strategies for answering each type of question:

Measuring Up® on Multiple-Choice Questions

A multiple-choice question has two parts. The first part is the question, or stem. It has a number in front of it. The second part is the choices, or answers. They have letters (A, B, C, D) with circles in front of them that you will fill in to choose the correct answer.

There are different kinds of multiple-choice questions. The first kind, in the vocabulary and informational sections, looks like this. Take note of the boldface words:

1. "George is a good soccer player. He scored 3 goals in the championship to help his team win. The team was awarded medals for their **accomplishment**."

   What does the word **accomplishment** mean?

   A. achievement

   B. achievable

   C. competition

   D. disappointment

To answer this type of question, you have to think about the word, and how it is used in the sentence. Read all the sentences carefully and look for context clues. Then look at all the word parts. Choose the answer choice that gives the best meaning of that word.

There is also another kind of question that is set up differently:

2. Why was Cindy rewarded?

   A. She worked very hard the whole school year.

   B. She worked very hard to find her lost dog.

   C. She worked very hard to get an A on her test.

   D. She worked very hard to write a letter.

To answer this type of question, you should go back to the selection and find where this information is written. Reread the entire paragraph, look for context clues, and choose the answer that best fits with the question.

Measuring Up® on Short-Response Questions

A short-response question also has different parts. First there is a question. Then there will be space for you to write in your answer. It is important that you understand exactly what the question is asking you to do. You will be graded on all parts of the question.

There are different kinds of short-response questions. The first kind looks like this:

4. Some scientists believe that **jets** of natural gas were the main cause for the explosion.

   jet /jet/ *n.* **1)** a forced stream. **2)** a kind of airplane. **3)** a type of coal. **4)** extremely dark black.

   Which dictionary definition is used to define **jets** in the sentence above? Use information from the story to support your answer.

   _____

   _____

To answer this type of question, go back to the story and figure out the context of the word. Be sure to use backup information as to why you made this choice.

Another kind of short-response question asks you to write in an answer booklet:

5. Write your answer in the **Answer Booklet**.

   How did Mary feel when she found out her dog Cindy ran away? Use information from the selection to support your answer.

To answer this type of question, think about how the information is related. Go back to the selection to help you answer the question. Then write your answers on the lines provided. Make sure you write your answers clearly.

There are important strategies for answering questions. Try these:

- Read each selection to find its subject and the main idea. You may look back at the reading selection as often as necessary.

- Read each question carefully. Think about what the question is asking you to do. If a graph or other type of diagram goes along with the question, be sure to look at it carefully. It is there to help you answer the question. Then choose or write the answer that you think is best.

- When you write your answers to the short- and extended-response questions, write them neatly and clearly in the space provided. If a grader cannot read it, it will be marked incorrect.

- When you are asked to select the answer in a multiple-choice question, make sure you fill in the circle next to the answer. Mark only one answer. If you have to erase a mark to change answers, be sure to erase it completely.

- If you do not know the answer to the question right away, skip it and continue on to the next question. Then if you have time later, go back to the questions you skipped and answer them before you hand in your test booklet.

- If you finish the test early, you may check over your work until time runs out.

- When you are finished and your test booklet has been collected, you may take out your silent work.

Strategies to Measure Up

There are some general test-preparation strategies you can use to succeed. Here are a few useful tips:

- Start getting ready now. Spend a few minutes a day practicing answers to test questions.

- Get a good night's sleep the night before the test.

- Eat a good breakfast.

- Remember the story of the little engine that kept saying, "I think I can. I think I can." Keep telling yourself that you will do well. Then you probably will. That's what it means to "think positively."

- Wear a watch. Keep track of time so that you finish the whole test.

Measuring Up® with Independent Practice for the Test

A special feature of Measuring Up® is Independent Practice for the Test. It was created to give you practice and build your confidence for taking hard tests. The more you practice answering hard questions, the more prepared you will be to succeed.

You will learn a lot in Measuring Up®. You will review and practice the Academic Content Standards. You will practice for the *Ohio Achievement Test*. Finally, you will build your stamina to answer tough questions. You will more than measure up. You'll be a smashing success!

Explanation of Standards Numbering System: The Ohio Academic Content Standards (Benchmarks and Grade Level Indicators) for Reading used in this Measuring Up® worktext have been given an identity code for quick recognition and useful simplicity for the Grade 5–specific reading objectives.

The coding system uses the following letters and numbers:

Sample code: LA-C-A-5.1

Language Arts: LA

Standards:

A Acquisition of Vocabulary

B Reading Process: Concepts of Print, Comprehension Strategies and Self-Monitoring Strategies

C Reading Applications: Informational, Technical and Persuasive Text

D Reading Applications: Literary Text

Benchmark: A. Use context clues and text structures to determine the meaning of new vocabulary.

Grade: 5

Grade Level Indicator: 1. Define the meaning of unknown words by using context clues and the author's use of definition, restatement and example.

Chapter 1 Word Analysis and Vocabulary Development

What's Coming Up?

In this chapter, you will learn how:

- to use context clues;
- to understand synonyms, antonyms, homophones, homonyms, and homographs;
- to understand connotation and denotation;
- to understand figurative language;
- to understand word origins and derivations;
- to understand prefixes, suffixes, and roots;
- to use resources to find word meaning.

Word Meaning

When you begin to read, you learn to sound out words. But words are more than their sounds. They also carry a great deal of meaning. Some words are familiar. You know their meaning right away. Some words are unfamiliar. You need to use content clues or word structure clues to figure out what they mean. Many words have multiple meanings. When you read words with multiple meanings, you must figure out which meaning is meant in the context. Knowing the meanings of words is a key to improving your comprehension.

Words Are All Around Us

Words are fascinating, and they are all around us. Many words have interesting stories to tell. These stories may explain how particular words traveled from Spain or France or China or Japan, for example, to become part of the English language. Others may be family stories. They tell how words are related since they are built from the same root. Other stories explain how words have changed in meaning over time. In this chapter, you will learn many of these remarkable stories about words.

Lesson 1

Strategies for Reading

Activity

Directions Look for words around you that are described below. Look through magazines, books, and newspapers. You can also listen for words in conversations, television shows, movies, and on the radio. Write your answers.

1. a word we use in English that comes from Spanish

   _____

2. the longest word you can find

   _____

3. the shortest word you can find

   _____ANT_____

4. a figurative expression that you really like

   _____

5. two synonyms or words that mean the same thing

   _____

6. a word with more than one prefix

   _____

7. a word with a suffix

   _____

8. a word we use in English that comes from French

   _____

9. a word based on the Latin root *phon*, which means sound

   _____

10. two words that sound alike but have different meanings

    _____here hear_____

LA-A-A-5.1, LA-A-B-5.2, LA-A-C-5.3, LA-A-D-5.4, LA-A-D-5.5, LA-A-E-5.6, LA-A-D-5.7, LA-A-F-5.8

Comprehension is the ability to get the appropriate meaning from written text. Reading requires word recognition. The strategies below will help you to recognize, read, and understand new words.

Keys To Success

  Use Context Clues

You can sometimes figure out the meaning of an unfamiliar word by looking at its context. **Context clues** may be words or sentences that help explain the unfamiliar word. Use context clues when you see a word you do not know.

  Understand Synonyms, Antonyms, Homophones, Homonyms, and Homographs

Some words cause confusion because they look alike or sound alike. **Synonyms** are words that have the same or almost the same meaning. For example, *big* and *large* are synonyms. **Antonyms** are words that have the opposite meaning. For example, *big* and *small* are antonyms. **Homophones** are words that sound alike but have different spellings and meanings. For example, *one* and *won* are homophones. Some people call them **homonyms**. **Homographs** are words that are spelled alike but have different meanings. They sometimes have different pronunciations. For example, you can tie a *bow* and you can take a *bow*.

  Understand Connotation and Denotation

You know words have meanings. When you define a word by its dictionary meaning, it is called its **denotation**. For example, *home* means "a place where you live." Some words also have a **connotation**. This refers to the feelings and memories that the word stirs up. For example, the word *home* suggests a place of comfort and protection.

 Understand Figurative Language

Sometimes you may read words that have a special meaning. For example, if you read the words "his teeth were like pearls," it would mean that the teeth were very white and sparkling. It doesn't literally mean that the teeth were made of pearls. This is known as **figurative language** and it is used to describe people, places, or things.

 Understand Word Origins and Derivations

The English language is made up of words from many different languages. Knowing the **history** of a word can help you better understand its meaning. It can also help you understand related words.

 Understand Prefixes, Suffixes, and Roots

Joining together different word parts forms many words. You can combine **prefixes**, **roots**, and **suffixes** to form words. Knowing the meaning of word parts can help you understand the meaning of the new words.

 Use Resources to Find Word Meaning

A **dictionary** tells you the meaning of a word. It also tells the word's pronunciation, part of speech, and word history. Look up words you don't know and can't find the meaning of by using context clues and word parts. Use a **thesaurus** to find synonyms and antonyms.

     Measuring Up® to the Ohio Academic Content Standards

READING GUIDE

GUIDED QUESTIONS

Directions Put your strategies to use as you read "Keeping Cool with Crickets." Use the questions in the margin to guide your reading.

1 Keeping Cool with Crickets
by Lois Jacobson

2 "*Konnichiwa*. Good afternoon," my Japanese neighbor called through the door. "I have brought you a present to welcome you to Japan.

The package was very small and tied with delicately curled ribbons. What could such a tiny box contain? Puzzled, I lifted the lid, and there, nestled in whisper-thin tissue paper, was a blue-and-white dish. It was **3** shaped like a miniature bottle cap, and its cracked, glazed surface made it look very old—and very special.

"It's a water dish for crickets." My new friend's voice almost chirped with delight.

"What does one do with a water dish for crickets?" I asked.

"You put it inside a cricket house."

"Cricket house?"

"If you are going to live in Tokyo during the heat of the summer," said my neighbor, "you must learn to keep cool with crickets!"

4 Now I was curious. I soon learned that in the Far East, people have kept crickets as pets for centuries. In the past they housed them in cages made of bamboo or delicately carved jade, which they hung from the eaves or porches of their weathered homes. Bamboo cages are still used today, but most children keep their crickets in plastic cages the colors of cool lime or raspberry sherbet.

1 Homographs The word *cricket* can refer to a game or a type of insect. What does it mean in this story? How do you know?

2 Synonyms Circle the word *present*. What is a synonym for *present* in this context?

3 Word Parts Circle the word part *mini* in *miniature*. Is a *miniature* box very large or very small? How do you know?

4 Word Parts Circle the word *centuries*. How many years are in a *century*? What part of a dollar is a *cent*? What do you think the word part *cent* means?

5 During the hot, breathless summer months, Japanese parks are filled with laughing children and parents, armed with butterfly nets and small towels, pursuing their prey. The crickets are hard to catch because their hind legs are well developed for jumping. But once trapped in a net or under a small towel, they can be put in cages or small glass jars with air holes in the lids.

6 For people who can't catch their own, there are cricket vendors. I soon found myself at a market stall eyeing a plump, brownish black cricket. The vendor put my selection in a cardboard container. From the vibrations, I knew that my cricket didn't like being shut up inside. He needed a house.

He and I scouted out the local cricket real-estate market. Our search ended in a cluttered stall filled with bamboo wares. Tucked in a corner, amid baskets and flower containers, was a miniature Japanese **7** house made of slender bamboo reeds. It was just right for the antique water dish—and, of course, for my cricket.

8 Using many hand gestures, the kimono-clad shopkeeper explained that the bottom of the house must be layered with just enough soil to anchor the filled water dish. Crickets, she added, love raw potatoes, cucumbers, bits of water-soaked bread, and leafy greens—all in cricket-sized portions.

Charlie and I were eager to move in. I knew he was **9** a Charlie because only male crickets chirp. Crickets have four wings that lie flat, one pair over the other on top of their bodies. By raising the upper pair of wings and rubbing one wing over the other, the males produce their singing or chirping sound.

5 **Homophones** Circle the word *prey*. What does it mean? What word sounds the same as *prey* but is spelled differently?

6 **Context Clues** Circle the word *vendors*. Use context clues to tell what a *vendor* does. Underline the words that helped you to understand the meaning of the word.

7 **Connotation** What does the word *antique* suggest to you?

8 **Word Origin and Dictionary** Circle the word *kimono*. Based on the context, from which language do you think the word comes from? Then define *kimono*. Use a dictionary.

9 **Homophones** Circle the word *pair*. What is a homophone for this word that means "a fruit"?

READING GUIDE

10 Each song has a meaning. Some serve as calling songs to attract females, others as courting songs to encourage mating or as fighting songs to repel other males. In Japan it is said that they sing, "*Kata sase suso samusa ga kuruzo*," or "Sew your sleeves, sew your skirts, the cold weather is coming."

Charlie Cricket was quiet as I put down a thin layer of dirt in his home, stocked his pantry with lettuce and potatoes, and added the antique water dish. Now, how was I going to get that bundle of energy from carton to house? I lifted the cardboard **11** flap, and Charlie eyed me, ready to do battle. Using all ten fingers, a soothing voice, and lots of encouragement, I soon had him safely in his house.

Drugged by the summer heat, I hung Charlie from **12** the eaves of the balcony. Nearby, wind chimes tinkled melodiously with each gentle breeze.

"Cool me off," I plead. "Chirp, Charlie, chirp." The heat hung suspended around me, And Charlie chirped!" The garden bells tinkled in accompaniment. **13** It was as if the enchanting sounds and the whirring of cricket wings awakened the air and stirred it about me ever so gently.

14 "Sing, Charlie!" His song sounded like the clinking of ice cubes in chilled crystal goblets. The heat seemed to waft away. I had learned the Japanese art of keeping cool with crickets.

GUIDED QUESTIONS

10 Antonyms and Context Circle the word *attract*. Find an antonym for *attract* in this sentence. What context clue helps you understand what this antonym means?

11 Word Parts Circle the word *encouragement*. What word part is added to the end of this word?

12 Word Parts Circle the word *melodiously*. What base word is used to form this longer word?

13 Figurative Language How does the author use figurative language to describe the air as alive?

14 Figurative Language How does the author use figurative language to compare the cricket's song? What impression or feeling does this create?

Use Context Clues

LA-A-A-5.1

What can you do when you read a word you do not know? Use **context** to figure out how the word is used in the sentence. Look for **context clues** in the words, sentences or even paragraphs that come before or after the unfamiliar word. These clues can help you figure out what the word means.

Here are five ways context can help you tell the meaning of a word.

Definition Sometimes a writer defines the word. For example,

> LeMar and Sandy attended a *jai alai* game. This is a game like handball, but it is played with a curved basket attached to the player's arm.

You may not know the meaning of *jai alai* when you started to read. However, the writer gives you a definition in the next sentence.

Restatement Sometimes a writer restates or puts in other words the meaning of the unfamiliar word. For example,

> Jaime was *resistant* to Sam's suggestion to go to the movie. In other words, he was dead-set against it.

You may not know the meaning of *resistant*. However, when you read that he was "dead-set against it" you know resistant means "opposed to" or "against."

Synonym Sometimes a writer provides a word that means the same or almost the same thing as the unfamiliar word. For example,

> Kristin was *jubilant* when she won the prize. She was so happy she felt like jumping up and down.

You may not know the meaning of *jubilant*. However, the word *happy* tells you that *jubilant* means "filled with joy" or "very happy."

Antonym Sometimes a writer provides a word that means the opposite of the unfamiliar word. For example,

> On the other hand, Keith was *despondent*. He did not feel happy like his sister Kristen did.

You may not know what *despondent* means. However, when you read that Keith "did not feel happy," you can figure out that *despondent* means "not happy" or "sad."

Example Sometimes a writer provides an example that shows what the word means.

> Hector is good at gymnastics because he is so *limber*. For example, he can bend over and touch his toes with his elbows and sit and put both feet behind his neck.

You may not know what *limber* means. However, the two examples described in the second sentence tell you that *limber* must mean "able to bend easily."

Activity

Directions Read the story below. Then answer the questions that follow it.

How Do Owls Hunt at Night?
by Edna Manning

There's a faint rustle in the dead leaves on the forest floor. A tiny mouse stops and peers around in the dim starlight, listening carefully. Without a sound, an owl swoops from the night sky. Amidst a swirl of leaves, the mouse becomes the owl's midnight snack.

Although some owls hunt during the day, most prefer to hunt at night. Nocturnal animals, such as owls, foxes, deer, and cats, have huge eyeballs that help to gather as much light as possible. The eye of the snowy owl is just as large as an adult human eye but is in a much smaller skull. If our eyes were that large for our body size, they'd be as big as oranges!

An owl also has excellent eyesight because its eyes face forward. This gives it very good binocular vision, meaning the view it sees with both eyes overlaps, just as a human's does. This kind of vision allows the owl to see three-dimensional objects, helping it figure out the distance from its perch on the tree to the mouse below. Try closing one eye. Then reach for an object an arm's length away. It's hard to know exactly how far to reach, isn't it? Owls can also shift focus from close up to far away very quickly. They can zoom in on a mouse 200 yards away.

Since the owl can't move its eyes in its sockets, it can look only straight ahead. An owl, however, has a very long and flexible neck. It can turn its head so far back it can see what's going on behind it without moving its body. In fact, an owl can move its head a full 270 degrees.

An owl's eyes are also good at making use of very little light. Some, like the tawny owl, can see in light

       Measuring Up® to the Ohio Academic Content Standard

Activity continued

100 times less bright than we can. The opening in the eye that lets in the light is called a pupil. At night the owl's pupils open very wide to let in as much light as possible. This results in a larger "picture" being made on the retina at the back of the eye. Think of the retina as the film in a camera where the picture is made.

The retina is made up of tiny cells called rods and cones that are sensitive to light. Cones react to bright light and colors. Rod cells are used in dim light for seeing at night, but they don't provide the ability to see color. For example, try finding a particular color of T-shirt in a dark closet. Pretty tough to do, huh? Nocturnal animals, such as owls, have more rods than cones, so they see well at night, but without much color. They don't need to know if the mouse is brown or gray.

Another feature of an owl's eyes that helps it make use of low light is called eyeshine. Have you noticed how the eyes of a cat or deer seem to glow at night? They, like the owl, have a mirrorlike layer called a tapetum behind the retina. Some light entering the eye passes through the retina without being absorbed by the cells. The tapetum reflects the light back into the eyes, giving the cells of the retina a second chance to absorb it. Even a small amount of light shining into the eyes will make them look like they're glowing. Whales, sharks, crocodiles, fruit-eating bats, and some snakes and birds also have this eyeshine.

Some people think owls can't see well during the day, this isn't true. Just as the pupils in our eyes adjust to the amount of light entering them, so do the owls' pupils. However, most animals that are active both during the day and at night have pupils that open very wide at night and close tight during the day to protect the sensitive cells from bright sunlight.

Many animals, including owls, combine their ability to see at night with their other keen senses to hunt and to avoid being hunted. And although owls must be pleased with their wonderful nighttime hunting skills, the mice probably don't appreciate those skills very much.

Activity continued

1. Read the paragraph below.

> An owl's eyes are also good at making use of very little light. Some, like the tawny owl, can see in light 100 times less bright than we can. The opening in the eye that lets in the light is called a pupil. At night the owl's pupils open very wide to let in as much light as possible. This results in a larger "picture" being made on the retina at the back of the eye. Think of the *retina* as the film in a camera where the picture is made.

   What is the definition of the word *pupil*?

   opening in eye is called pupil

2. How does the author use context clues to help you to understand the meaning of *retina*?

   Film of a camera

   _____

3. If you didn't know the word *tapetum*, you could figure it out from context clues. What is tapetum?

   middle like layer
   behind the RETINA

Activity continued

4. Read the paragraph below.

> Another feature of an owl's eyes that helps it make use of low light is called *eyeshine*. Have you noticed how the eyes of a cat or deer seem to glow at night? They, like the owl, have a mirrorlike layer called a *tapetum* behind the retina. Some light entering the eye passes through the retina without being absorbed by the cells. The tapetum reflects the light back into the eyes, giving the cells of the retina a second chance to absorb it. Even a small amount of light shining into the eyes will make them look like they're glowing. Whales, sharks, crocodiles, fruit-eating bats, and some snakes and birds also have this eyeshine.

In your own words, write a definition for *eyeshine*. Tell what it is and how it helps an owl to see. Use context clues.

sun glows in your eyes!!

5. Look at paragraph 6, Explain how *cones* are different from *rods*.

CONes - react to Bright Light

Rod cells - use in dim light

Apply to the Test

Directions: Use the story you just read to answer questions 1–5.

1. Read the sentences below.

   There's a faint **rustle** in the dead leaves on the forest floor. A tiny mouse stops and peers around in the dim starlight, listening carefully.

   Which words below best help you understand the meaning of the word **rustle**?

   A. dead leaves

   B. forest floor

   C. tiny mouse

   D. listens carefully

2. As used in this article, what does **binocular** mean?

   A. good eyesight

   B. from one eye only

   C. seeing with both eyes

   D. seeing straight ahead

3. Read the sentences below.

Although some owls hunt during the day, most prefer to hunt at night. **Nocturnal** animals, such as owls, foxes, deer, and cats, have huge eyeballs that help to gather as much light as possible.

Which context clue best helps you figure out the meaning of **nocturnal**?

A. at night

B. owls

C. during the day

D. huge eyeballs

4. Read the sentences below.

An owl, however, has a very long and **flexible** neck. It can turn its head so far back it can see what's going on behind it without moving its body. In fact, an owl can move its head a full 270 degrees.

What is the meaning of the word **flexible**?

A. having a long neck

B. able to bend or turn easily

C. very tight and rigid

D. not able to move

5. Owls are good hunters. Explain two special features of its eyes that help it hunt prey. Write your answer on a separate sheet of paper.

A **synonym** is a word that means the same or almost the same as another word. For example, the words *decorated* and *ornate* are synonyms. So are the words *sad* and *gloomy*.

An **antonym** is a word that means the opposite of another word. For example, the words *tame* and *wild* are antonyms. So are the words *narrow* and *wide*.

When you read, look for synonyms and antonyms. They can help you determine the meaning of unfamiliar words. For example, read the sentence below.

> The rain *pounded* the roof and *buffeted* the window.

You may not know the meaning of the word *buffeted*. Its synonym is *pounded*. This tells you that *buffeted* means "hit hard." Another synonym is *battered*.

Now look at this sentence.

> The next day began in just the opposite way. Instead of *ferocious* winds, a *gentle* breeze blew through the trees.

You may not know the meaning of *ferocious*. Its antonym is *gentle*, so *ferocious* means "fierce" or "not gentle."

Homophones are words that sound alike but are spelled differently and have different meanings. For example, the words *seem* and *seam* are homophones. *Seem* means "appear" and *seam* means "the line formed by sewing cloth together." Some people call these **homonyms**.

Homographs are words that are spelled the same but have different meanings and usually different word histories. For example, you can save money in a *bank* and you can sit on the *bank* of a river. Sometimes the words have different pronunciations. For example, *wind* a clock and the *wind* that blew her hat away. Be sure to use the context of the sentence or paragraph the word is in to help you determine the correct meaning of a homograph.

Activity

Directions Read the story below. Then answer the questions that follow it.

Fabulous Frederic
by Peggy Thorne

My show was terrific—right up until the last trick.

I had a wooden stage, a top hat, and my uncle Herbert's wand. I pulled quarters out of kids' ears and a stuffed rabbit out of my hat. I read my brother Theodore's mind. I made a stream of colored confetti shoot out of my wand, and I made a baseball float across the stage. Around twenty-five people were in the audience, most of them kids from the neighborhood. I had them on the edge of their seats.

But my last trick was my greatest, my most stupendous.

What I mean is, it was supposed to be great.

It's a complicated card trick I call the Color Switch. It's not the fanciest trick I know, but from a magician's point of view, it's the hardest.

When I announced the trick, I saw Uncle Herbert straighten up and fix his eyes on my hands. He used to be a professional magician, so he knew exactly where to look.

There was only one problem: the Color Switch didn't work.

You see, this trick depends on sleight of hand. I have two decks of cards that I have to switch—*without* the audience seeing. I'd practiced the trick a lot, of course, but I couldn't do it as well as my other tricks. In fact, I only got it right about three-quarters of the time. (The first rule of being a magician is never to perform a trick that's not perfectly prepared, but I really wanted to impress my uncle.)

Anyway, the worst thing that could possibly happen did happen: the hidden deck fell out of my sleeve when I was making the switch. So there they were, fifty-two cards the audience wasn't supposed to see, spilled all over the stage.

Everybody laughed.

Activity continued

I tried to put on a good face, which is what you have to do when something goes wrong. I made a joke and smiled confidently when I took my bows. Then I called Theodore out for a bow. He's a really good sport, which is why he agreed to be my assistant for the mind-reading trick. Incredible as it might seem, he'd rather draw pictures than do magic. Theodore is my identical twin, but my dad always says you couldn't find two people more different *anywhere*.

After the show, Theodore and Uncle Herbert helped me clean up. Uncle Herbert told me I'd done a terrific job, which I knew was basically true, and then asked me to do the sleight of hand for the card trick I goofed up.

I did it for him, and it worked pretty well, but Uncle Herbert just shook his head. "Not smooth enough for palming cards. If you keep practicing, though, you'll be able to do that trick expertly—in another four years or so."

Four years. That was a discouraging thought.

I looked at Uncle Herbert's hands. They're big and long-fingered. As the Fabulous Franzetti, sleight of hand tricks had been his specialty. I can remember seeing him brush his hand across a table and make an entire deck of cards disappear—just like magic. That was years ago, before his arthritis got bad enough that he'd had to retire.

The Fabulous Franzetti was looking at me kindly. "Maybe you should play to your strengths," he said.

"My strengths?"

"You have something very special—something almost no other magician has." Then he nodded his head at my brother, Theodore.

I looked at Theodore and knew exactly what Uncle Herbert was thinking. "It wouldn't work," I said. "Everybody in the neighborhood knows us."

"Your show is terrific—good enough to take on the road. In fact, I have an excellent idea where you could start."

     Measuring Up® to the Ohio Academic Content Standard

So that's how Fabulous Frederic's Magnificent Magic Show wound up at the Glenville Retirement Home. It had a big auditorium with a real stage. About a hundred people showed up; I was thrilled.

I did the same show I'd done in my backyard, with two differences. First, instead of reading my brother's mind, I read my sister Amanda's. She wore her silver gymnastics outfit, and the crowd loved her.

Second, I replaced the Color Switch with Instant Teleportation. My new trick worked like this: I wheeled a coatrack with a black velvet curtain out to the center of the stage. I pulled the curtain aside to show the audience there was nothing behind it. Then I stepped past it with a showy twirl of my cape and snapped the curtain shut behind me.

My father was waiting at the back of the auditorium. As soon as I snapped the curtain shut, he rang a bell and set off a camera flash. The noise and the light made everybody turn to the back of the auditorium. Then Theodore stepped into the aisle. He was dressed exactly like me, and of course everybody thought he *was* me.

He bowed to the crowd, then walked down to the stage. Everyone stared at him, while I stepped back from the coatrack and disappeared backstage. When Theodore reached the stage, he grandly pulled the curtain aside to show that no one was there.

The crowd went wild. From their point of view, it looked like I had stepped behind the curtain and then instantly appeared at the back of the auditorium.

Amanda ran up onstage with Theodore then, and the two of them took their bows. Everybody stood up and clapped, which didn't surprise me. It was a great trick.

I was backstage, of course, while Theodore and Amanda were getting all the applause, but that didn't matter. The Fabulous Franzetti patted me on the back and told me he was glad I was using his wand. That was enough for me.

Activity continued

1. Read the sentence below.

   What I *mean* is, it was supposed to be great.

   The word *mean* can be defined as
   - intend or want to express;
   - bad-tempered or not kind;
   - average or in the middle.

   What is its meaning in the sentence above? Write a sentence using *mean* with one of the other meanings.

   _____

   _____

2. Read the paragraph below.

   It's a *complicated* card trick I call the Color Switch. It's not the fanciest trick I know, but from a magician's point of view, it's the hardest.

   What is a synonym for *complicated*? What is an antonym?

   _____

   _____

3. Read the sentence below.

   Theodore is my *identical* twin, but my dad always says you couldn't find two people more *different anywhere*.

   Are *identical* and *different* synonyms, homographs, or antonyms? Write a sentence using each word.

   _____

   _____

   Measuring Up® to the Ohio Academic Content Standard

Activity continued

4. Read the paragraph below.

When I announced the trick, I saw Uncle Herbert *straighten* up and fix his *eyes* on my hands. He used to *be* a professional magician, *so* he *knew* exactly *where* to look.

Here's a challenge. Find a homophone for each word below. Tell what each means. (For one of the words, find two homophones.)

	Homophone	Meaning
A straight (not crooked)	_____	_____
B eye (one of two organs that helps you see)	_____	_____
	_____	_____
C be (exist)	_____	_____
D so (as a result]	_____	_____
E knew (understood)	_____	_____
F where (what place)	_____	_____

Activity continued

5. Read the sentence below.

(The first rule of being a magician is never to perform a trick that's not perfectly prepared, but I really wanted to *impress* my uncle.)

The word *impress* can mean
- to force someone into service;
- to make someone think a lot of you.

What does *impress* mean in the sentence above? What is a synonym you could use for it in this sentence? What is an antonym?

_____

_____

 **Apply to the Test**

Directions: Use the story you just read to answer questions 1–5.

1. The main character is called "Fabulous Frederic." All of the following are synonyms from the story for **fabulous** except

   A. terrific.

   B. terrible.

   C. greatest.

   D. stupendous.

2. "I pulled **quarters** out of kids' ears and a stuffed rabbit out of my hat."

   Which meaning best fits the word **quarters** in the sentence above?

   A. four equal parts of something

   B. coins that are worth 25 cents

   C. the legs of an animals

   D. placed where soldiers are lodged

3. "You see, this trick depends on **sleight** of hand."

   Which sentence below uses one of the homophones **sleight** and **slight** correctly.

   A. He had a **sleight** build for a wrestler.

   B. The magician was known for his **slight** of hand, or skill.

   C. The sick child had a **sleight** fever.

   D. There is only a **slight** chance of rain tomorrow.

4. "Amanda ran up onstage with Theodore then, and the two of them took their **bows**."

   In the sentence above, **bow** means

   A. movement bending the upper body to accept applause.

   B. front part of a ship.

   C. knot with loops.

   D. curved piece of wood for shooting arrows.

5. Retell how Frederic performs his Instant Teleportation trick. Write your answer on a separate sheet of paper.

When you define a word, you tell its dictionary meaning. The exact meaning of a word is its **denotation**.

When you tell about the feelings and emotions that a word stirs up, you tell its **connotation**. The impression a word conveys is its connotation. The impression can be positive or negative. For example, look at the sentences below.

> The waves *washed* onto the beach, *scattering* their cool spray across the pebbles.
>
> The waves *crashed* onto the beach, *flinging* their cool spray across pebbles.

The words *washed* and *crashed* both mean almost the same, "a flow or rush of water." That's their denotation. The first sentence has a positive impression because the word *washed* implies a gentle movement. The second sentence expresses a negative feeling because the word *crashed* implies a strong force. That's their connotation.

Now look at the words *scattering* and *flinging* in the sentences above. These words mean almost the same, but they stir up different emotions. Which word has a negative connotation? Why? Yes, it is the word *flinging* because it implies throwing something.

Both denotation and connotation are important. When you write and speak, choose words that express both the meaning and the impression you wish to convey. For example, when you were younger, you probably read books about Curious George. Do you think the books about this inquisitive monkey would have been as popular if the author had called him Prying George?

Activity

Directions Read the second part of the selection below. Then answer the questions that follow it.

from **Small Dog Blues**
by Bonnie Brightman

The living room was cold when Ricky got up early Sunday morning to watch TV. He laid his sleeping bag on the floor and crawled in. The little Chihuahua crawled in, too. It scrambled to the bottom of the bag and curled itself around Ricky's feet.

"You're a pretty good heater," Ricky said into his sleeping bag. The dog snored happily. "It's nothing personal, you know," Ricky went on, feeling guilty about his plan to give the dog back. "You're going to be a great dog for the right person." The dog snored some more. Ricky smiled and turned back to his program.

The next afternoon, Ricky put on his jacket to take the dog for a walk. The thermometer outside the living room window read zero. Ricky looked worriedly at the dog sitting patiently by the door.

"Ricky, look what I made for your friend," said Abuela. "It's a sweater! Isn't it cute?" she asked, holding it up for Ricky to see. It was bright red with navy blue tassels hanging from the neck.

Ricky looked from the weather to the Chihuahua. Sweaters were for sissy dogs only. Even Ricky would not wear a sweater if he could get away with it. On the other hand, it was cold outside, and he could not always carry the dog under his armpit.

"I know it's embarrassing, fella," he said to the Chihuahua as he pulled the sweater over its head and pushed it out the door. "But you'll freeze solid if you don't wear something."

It was a quiet, cold afternoon. Anybody with a warm place to go was inside. This suited Ricky fine. If no one was out, no one would ask him why he was walking a chicken in a sweater. Yes, this would work out O.K. Tomorrow he'd be getting a big dog—something that he could name Lobo—and this little temporary dog would find a good home. Maybe a home with some nice abuela.

Activity continued

"So that's what you had in your jacket yesterday!" boomed a voice. Ricky had not heard Steve and el Toro coming up behind him.

"Yeah, so?" asked Ricky, startled. Despite the cold, Ricky began to sweat as el Toro circled the Chihuahua, curling back his lips and showing his teeth. But before Ricky could scoop up the Chihuahua, it leaned toward the big dog and started to yip fiercely. El Toro sat down and wagged his tail.

"That's a cool little dog you've got there, Ricky," Stevie said.

"Well," Ricky answered proudly, "he's a Chihuahua. Chihuahuas were the royal dogs of Mexico, you know. They're known for their bravery."

"It must be nice to have a dog that doesn't pull you over all the time," Stevie said, shooting a look at el Toro.

"They're good heaters, too," Ricky answered. He picked the Chihuahua up and tucked it inside his jacket. The little dog popped its head out under Ricky's chin and looked el Toro straight in the eye.

"Actually," Ricky admitted, "I was pretty surprised when I first got it. I thought it'd be a lot . . . well . . . different."

The two boys continued walking their dogs together.

"What's its name?" asked Stevie.

"Lobo," said Ricky.

         Measuring Up® to the Ohio Academic Content Standard

Activity continued

1. Read the paragraph below.

   "You're a pretty good heater," Ricky said into his sleeping bag. The dog snored happily. "It's nothing personal, you know," Ricky went on, feeling guilty about his plan to give the dog back. "You're going to be a great dog for the right person." The dog snored some more. Ricky smiled and turned back to his program.

   Look carefully at the words in this paragraph. How do you know that Ricky's feelings toward the dog are beginning to change?

   _____

   _____

2. Read the sentence below.

   Ricky looked worriedly at the dog sitting *patiently* by the door.

   The word *patiently* means "without complaining or making a fuss." Suppose the author had used the word *meekly* instead. Would the impression have been as positive? Explain.

   _____

   _____

   _____

Activity continued

3. Read the sentence below.

   "So that's what you had in your jacket yesterday!" boomed a voice.

   Why does the author use the word *boomed* instead of *shouted*? What does it suggest about how big and powerful Steve and his dog seem to Ricky?

   _____

   _____

   _____

4. Read the sentence below.

   "Yeah, so?" asked Ricky, *startled*.

   Use a thesaurus or dictionary to find three synonyms for *startled*. Which one carries the closest connotations to *startled*?

   _____

   _____

5. Use a thesaurus or dictionary to find three pairs of synonyms. One word in each pair should have positive connotations (for example, *slender*). One word should have negative connotations (for example, *scrawny*).

   _____

   _____

   _____

 Measuring Up® to the Ohio Academic Content Standards

Apply to the Test

Directions: Use the selection you just read to answer questions 1–5.

1. "The living room was cold when Ricky got up early Sunday morning to watch TV. He laid his sleeping bag on the floor and crawled in. The little Chihuahua crawled in, too. It **scrambled** to the bottom of the bag and **curled** itself around Ricky's feet."

    In the paragraph above, the words **scrambled** and **curled** make the dog seem

    A. cute and cuddly.

    B. pitiful and wretched.

    C. mean and aggressive.

    D. annoying and bothersome.

2. "'I know it's embarrassing, **fella**,' he said to the Chihuahua as he pulled the sweater over its head and pushed it out the door."

    When Ricky calls the dog **fella**, you know that

    A. he is very embarrassed by the dog.

    B. he is angry at the dog.

    C. he plans to return the dog .

    D. he is warming up toward the dog.

3. "But before Ricky could scoop up the Chihuahua, it leaned toward the big dog and started to **yip** fiercely."

    Which of the synonyms for **bark** would be the best replacement for **yip** in the sentence above?

    A. howl

    B. yap

    C. growl

    D. snarl

4. "The little dog **popped** its head out under Ricky's chin and looked el Toro straight in the eye."

    What impression is created by the word **popped** in the sentence above?

    A. The little dog is fierce.

    B. The little dog is frightened.

    C. The little dog is appealing.

    D. The little dog is hungry.

5. At the end of the story, why does Ricky decide to call the dog Lobo? Give two details from the story to support your response.

    _____

    _____

     Measuring Up® to the Ohio Academic Content Standards

Understand Figurative Language

LA-A-D-5.4

Do words always mean exactly what they say? Not always! **Figurative language** is language that is not meant to be taken literally. It is meant to create pictures in a reader's mind, to stir your imagination, and to help you see things in new and surprising ways. Figurative language is a figure of speech. Writers use three types of figurative language very often. They are similes, metaphors, and personification.

A **simile** is a comparison between two unlike things that uses the word *like* or *as*. For example,

> She was as cute *as* a button.
>
> Her brown eyes shined *like* the sun.

A **metaphor** is a comparison between two unlike things. It does not use the word *like* or *as*. For example,

> Memories are old movies that play over and over in my head.
>
> I am peanut butter and my best friend is jelly.

Personification means giving human qualities to nonhuman things, such as nature, animals, objects, or feelings. For example,

> The clouds cried.
>
> The chair said "ouch" when I sat down.

Writers also use **symbolism** to express ideas in their writing. For example, a rainbow can symbolize good luck while a bluebird can symbolize happiness.

Pause to figure out the meaning of figurative language as you read. Be aware of how figures of speech help you to form images of what you are reading.

Activity

Directions Read the selection below. Then answer the questions that follow it.

from **The Clarinet**
by Glenn Dixon

Everyone is looking at me. I am behind Mr. Cobble, standing in the dark beside the chairs. Very comfortable chairs for listening. Hundreds of chairs only for listening to music.

Mr. Cobble stops, hitting the music stand with his baton like hitting a horse. He shakes his head and begins to yell. But when he sees the eyes are not looking at him, he turns slowly, and I feel very small among all the empty chairs.

"You," he begins. "Who are you?" His voice is shaking with anger.

"Qing Ly," I say, using my true name so that he cannot make the sound.

"Why are you not playing?" He is, of course, seeing the empty chair beside Marianne.

"I need some air, sir."

"You need some air? Of course you need some air." He turns again to the orchestra. "You all need some air." He is yelling, louder than the trumpets. "You are playing Beethoven . . . Beethoven, do you hear? He must be played with force, with passion."

I am hurrying back up to my chair in the clarinet section and I am thinking, What is this word "passion"?

"You must lose the polite ideas you have, this skinny, pathetic air. Rage, rage . . . fill the music with rage!"

I can see the angry red in Mr. Cobble's face. His eyes are big like eggs, but he does not look at me.

"Again," he says, lifting up his baton. "From the beginning."

At supper I am telling Marianne I will not go to evening rehearsal. "But you must," she insists. Her eyes are large with tears. "You have to."

Measuring Up® to the Ohio Academic Content Standards

Activity continued

She is a nice girl, Marianne, but a little foolish. She is thinking that if I am not there, she will receive a double anger from Mr. Cobble. I do not care. I cannot play anymore in his anger. It is like blowing snow through my clarinet. My lips are like wood, and my fingers are like rock.

It is still light when everyone goes for the evening rehearsal. I stay in my room until they are gone and then, in the quiet, I go with my own clarinet case out into the evening.

We are in cabins here, and the woods are all around. The sky is a funny blue, and there is pink in the clouds. The evening is very, very long here in the summer. The sun is still swimming above the mountains, but the shadows are very big. My own shadow is as long as a tree.

The birds are watching me carefully as I walk quickly up into the high mountains. The path is smooth to begin, then becomes small with rocks and roots so that I must watch my steps carefully. I walk for an hour until I am very far away.

Finally I come to a bench on the path. I sit and look down on a beautiful valley. I can see the river and the highway far, far away.

It is cold here but very quiet. Everything is waiting for me to play. The trees and the mountains are waiting. I open my case and put my clarinet together.

I feel the bamboo of my father's reed on my lip, and my fingers become a part of the clarinet. The valves are moving my fingers. The clarinet is taking the air from me. And it comes, the music.

The long, sad notes of Mr. Mozart come from my clarinet. The mountain air is fat with them, and the branches of the trees dance in time, conducting me. It is music for a mountain place.

Mr. Mozart was also from the mountains. From Salzburg in Europe. They are mountains very far away from here, but I think they have Christmas trees also. So, it is right. I am correct in introducing the Clarinet Concerto in A by Mr. Wolfgang Mozart. These mountains are liking it very much.

Activity continued

I make many mistakes in the difficult parts, and in the parts where the orchestra plays, I take a breath and hear them in my imagining. When I am finished, I hear no applause. The trees are quiet, and the mountains are sleeping. But when I stand up, taking my clarinet apart to fit it into the case, I see a star in the western sky. It is so funny. It is still light, but there is a star in the sky.

This star is smiling at me. Smiling like my father. And I think that I am the only person in the world who can see it. I think that for this one time, this shining star is just for me.

1. Read this paragraph.

   Mr. Cobble stops, hitting the music stand with his baton like hitting a horse. He shakes his head and begins to yell. But when he sees the eyes are not looking at him, he turns slowly, and I feel very small among all the empty chairs.

   What is Kim saying about Mr. Cobble by comparing his action to hitting a horse?

   _____

   _____

2. Read the sentences below.

   It is like blowing snow through my clarinet. My lips are like wood, and my fingers are like rock.

   What is Kim trying to tell the reader by using these comparisons?

   _____

   _____

Activity continued

3. Read the paragraph below.

> We are in cabins here, and the woods are all around. The sky is a funny blue, and there is pink in the clouds. The evening is very, very long here in the summer. The sun is still swimming above the mountains, but the shadows are very big. My own shadow is as long as a tree.

Why does Kim compare her shadow to a tree?

_____

_____

4. Read the paragraph below.

> The long, sad notes of Mr. Mozart come from my clarinet. The mountain air is fat with them, and the branches of the trees dance in time, conducting me. It is music for a mountain place.

How are the trees dancing? In what way are they conducting Kim? What effect is created by this comparison?

_____

_____

_____

5. Reread the last paragraph in the selection. Find and write the sentence that uses personification. How does this sentence tell you about Kim?

_____

_____

Apply to the Test

Directions: Use the selection you just read to answer questions 1–5.

1. "His eyes are big like eggs."

   Kim uses a simile to suggest that

   A. Mr. Cobble's eyes are watery, but he is deliciously handsome.

   B. Mr. Cobble's eyes are bulging from strong emotion.

   C. Mr. Cobble is a Grade A musician who wants to spice up the music.

   D. Mr. Cobble believes that you have to crack a few eggs to make an omelette.

2. "I feel the bamboo of my father's reed on my lip, and my fingers become a part of the clarinet. The valves are moving my fingers. The clarinet is taking the air from me. And it comes, the music."

   When Kim says "my fingers become part of the clarinet," she is suggesting that

   A. a clarinet cannot have its feelings hurt.

   B. she is uncomfortable playing music.

   C. playing music is natural to her.

   D. her fingers are actually turning into a clarinet.

Copying is illegal.   Measuring Up® to the Ohio Academic Content Standards

3. "The long, sad notes of Mr. Mozart come from my clarinet. The mountain air is fat with them, and the branches of the trees dance in time, conducting me. It is music for a mountain place."

   How is the mountain air fat?

   A. Music fills the air.

   B. The air is humid and filled with moisture.

   C. The clouds are puffy.

   D. The air has swallowed Mr. Cobble's rage.

4. "Mr. Mozart was also from the mountains. From Salzburg in Europe. They are mountains very far away from here, but I think they have Christmas trees also. So, it is right. I am correct in introducing the Clarinet Concerto in A by Mr. Wolfgang Mozart. These mountains are liking it very much."

   What is Kim expressing when she says, "These mountains are liking it very much?"

   A. She is so lonely that she imagines that the mountains are her friends.

   B. Only she hears the beauty of Mozart's music.

   C. The music fits well in this place.

   D. The mountains are better critics than Mr. Cobble.

5. What does Mr. Cobble really mean when he tells the students to "fill the music with rage?" Write your answer on a separate sheet of paper.

Words often have very interesting histories. Many English words come from other languages such as Greek, Latin, French, and Spanish. In fact, it has been estimated that nearly 75 percent of the words in English are derived from Greek or Latin.

From ancient times to the present, human beings have traveled around the globe. Often, they settle in lands far from their birth. When people travel and settle down in a new land, they bring their languages with them. So, the main language of North America, the United States, became English, the language of England. But some words we consider English really come from other languages. These words, in part, tell the story of our history of many people from many cultures.

For example, the word **prose** comes from a Latin phrase that means "direct speech." When you do not speak or write poetry, you speak or write prose—ordinary language. The word *bugle* means "small trumpet without keys or valves." The word comes from the Latin word *buculus*, meaning "young ox." Long ago bugles were made from the horns of ox.

Have you ever worn a pair of moccasins? These are shoes made from soft leather. The word *moccasin* comes from a word in Algonquin, which is a Native-American language. Have you ever taken a ride in a *canoe*? That is a boat carved out of a tree trunk. The word *canoe* comes from Haiti, a Caribbean Island. Maybe you have been on a *yacht*, which is a large ship. The word originally meant "a ship used for chasing in order to catch," and that meaning comes from a Dutch word. The Dutch people were early settlers in the Northeastern United States. Perhaps you have had lunch on a *patio* and eaten *tacos* and *tortillas*. These words derive from Spanish.

Many words are derived from the same original Latin or Greek word. This means they have the same word root. For example, the word root *-pend* is a Latin root that means "hang." It forms the words *appendix*, *suspend*, and *pendulum*.

You can find more about word histories in a dictionary. Usually, the derivation of the word is provided at the beginning or the end of each entry. Sometimes it is set off in a special box, and it is usually abbreviated.

Directions Read the selection below. Then answer the questions that follow it.

E is for ENCYCLOPEDIA
by Charles W. Ferguson

As everyone knows, you can learn something about almost everything in an encyclopedia. You can also learn many things from the word itself. It is made up of words that talk to each other, and as you study them they tell a story of how parents feel about their children and how through the years adults want to share what they know.

The chief little word in the big word is *cyclo*. *Cyclo* is from the Greek word for circle: *kyklos*. You can recognize *cyclo* in words we use every day: in *bicycle* (having two wheels), *tricycle* (having three wheels), *motorcycle* (a contraption with cycles or wheels turned by a motor). You will find *cyclo* in the dreadful word *cyclone*, which tells you of a storm that moves in a circle. And you'll find it in those awful-looking giants of Greek mythology called Cyclops. These giants had only one eye and it was very big and very round, right in the middle of the forehead.

In encyclopedia, *cyclo* describes a circle men have tried to draw around knowledge. It goes all around and includes everything. Or tries to. The wish of men to get all facts in one circle is very old. The first attempt we know about was made by a Roman named Pliny the Elder, who died A.D. 79. His *Natural History* was in thirty-seven volumes. It included as much as he could put together not only about science but also about art and other things of his day.

Since Pliny men have been trying to keep information in a circle and make orbits around it. And one reason they have done it is that they want to share what they know with the mind that wants to know. For there is another important word besides *cyclo*. It is *paideia*, meaning education, and this in turn is drawn out of another Greek word—the most important of all. This is *pais*, meaning child.

Activity continued

So in origin as well as fact an encyclopedia is a thing to teach a child about everything. It is a book for children in that men want to pass on what they have learned and keep it neat for others.

Of course what they have learned gets bigger and bigger all the time. One professor says our body of facts has doubled in the past fifty years and will double again in the next ten. So the task of drawing a circle around it gets harder and harder, and now we have special encyclopedias of this and that, encircling small fields of special information. And even they are getting big. There's no telling where it will all end. Perhaps in an encyclopedia of encyclopedias.

1. What does the author mean when he writes that the word *encyclopedia* is made up of words that talk to each other?

   _____

   _____

2. The author gives several words that come from the Greek word for *cycle: kyklos*. What are they? Use your dictionary to find at least one additional word.

   _____

   _____

   _____

3. Based on the word history, why do you think a *cyclone* is also called a twister?

   _____

   _____

Activity continued

4. Do you think it is possible to get all knowledge in one place? Explain.

_____

_____

_____

_____

5. The word *education* comes from the Latin word *ducere* meaning "to lead." Think about what education does and explain its connection to the word *lead*.

_____

_____

Apply to the Test

Directions: Use the selection you just read to answer questions 1–5.

1. What idea connects the words **cyclone**, **bicycle**, and **Cyclops** with the Greek word **kyklos**?

   A. a kind of power

   B. words that begin with the /k/ sound

   C. things that touch the ground

   D. a circle

2. How does the idea behind the word **kyklos** relate to the idea of an encyclopedia?

    A. Encyclopedias draw a circle around knowledge.

    B. Ancient encyclopedias were written on circular paper.

    C. Encyclopedias travel with men and women.

    D. Encyclopedias can be as dangerous as cyclones.

3. How does the idea behind the word **pais** relate to the idea of an encyclopedia?

    A. Receiving knowledge is like receiving pay.

    B. Encyclopedias teach children.

    C. **Pais** is the Greek name for **Pliny**.

    D. Children originally wrote encyclopedias

4. How does the idea behind the word **paideia** relate to the idea of an encyclopedia?

    A. Pupils wrote the encyclopedias of the past.

    B. Like feet that pedal bicycles, encyclopedias are on the move.

    C. Encyclopedias present knowledge.

    D. Encyclopedias are meant to circle the globe.

5. How do you think the Internet, or Information Highway, will change over the next 20 years? Provide two examples. Write your answer on a separate sheet of paper.

You can determine the meaning of unfamiliar words by using your knowledge of **prefixes**, **suffixes**, and **roots**.

A **prefix** is a word part or group of letters that is added to the beginning of a word and changes the word's meaning. When a prefix is added to a word it forms a new word.

Here are some common prefixes and their meanings.

Prefix	Meaning	Example
extra-	more than, beyond	**extra**ordinary
im-, in-	not	**im**pass
inter-	between	**inter**state
mis-	badly, wrong	**mis**behave
non-	not	**non**descript
post-	after, later	**post**pone
sub-	under, less important, a part or division of, near	**sub**way
super-	beyond, more, higher in rank	**super**star

A **suffix** is a word part with a specific meaning that is added to the end of a base word. A suffix can change a base word's meaning or its part of speech. Spelling changes can occur when suffixes are added. Here are some common suffixes and their meanings.

Suffix	Meaning	Example	Part of Speech
-al	relating to	manu**al**	adjective
-ive	tending to, having the nature of	creat**ive**	adjective
-less	without	care**less**	adjective
-ment	act of, result of, state of	achieve**ment**	noun
-ness	state or quality of	clean**ness**	noun
-tion	act of, state of, result of	imagina**tion**	noun
-ure	state of, act of	nat**ure**	noun
-y	state or quality of	funn**y**, ic**y**	adjective

A **root** is a word part that has meaning but cannot stand alone. A prefix or suffix may be added to a root to form a new word and change its meaning. For example, the word *cred* means "believe." You can add a suffix to it to form *credible*, which means "believable." Here are some roots from Latin and Greek and their meanings.

Root	Meaning	Example
cap, cept	take	ac**cept**
cit	call, start	ex**cit**ement
cred	believe	**cred**ible
fid	faith, trust	con**fid**ent
pel, pulse	drive, urge	re**pulse**
nat	born, spring forth	**nat**ure
sist, stit, stet	stand	re**sist**
ven, vent	come	ad**vent**ure

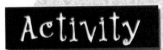

Directions Read the selection below. Then answer the questions that follow it.

Superheroes and Mischievous Imps
by Randall Lewis

When I was twelve, I often daydreamed. I escaped the humdrum of my everyday life by turning off my conscious mind. Instead, I let my subconscious mind go to work. Hopes and dreams that seemed buried came to the surface. Instead of thinking about homework and chores, I dreamt up superheroes and mischievous imps.

The superheroes were always saving the world. They used their superhuman power to do good. They worked nonstop to support bridges that were falling, stop avalanches from burying people, and held back tidal waves that were crashing to shore. They were the good guys of my imaginary life.

Activity continued

For every superhero, there was a supervillain. Although human, the supervillains did terrible deeds of extraordinary proportions. They would try to stop the world from turning, blot out the sun, and turn the oceans into solid ice.

The interaction between the superhero and the supervillain is what caused fun in my stories. When Mr. Misconduct tried to disable every plane in the sky, Windman blew a breath so strong it held them all up. When the Human Torpedo tried to hit a submarine, Ms. Marvel intercepted it in its path.

The imps, on the other hand, were always up to mischief. They were the misfits of my imaginary world. They didn't fit in with humans, so they played tricks on them whenever they had a chance. They turned princes into frogs. They put beautiful maidens into long sleeps. They carried people off to magical kingdoms from which they could never come back. They were little mean guys with supernatural powers that they used to misbehave in a big way.

Of course, they misbehaved in little ways, too. My imps loved doing lesser deeds just out of spite. They stole the homework you spent hours doing. They hid the house keys just as you were hurrying out the door. They gave you a "bad hair day" whenever there was an important party.

The imps, though, were always tricked by their own meanness. Once an imp turned a big, strong man into a stone. He placed the stone high over the cave where he lived. He liked to look up at that stone and laugh at the mischief he had done. His misdeeds delighted him. But after five years, the spell began to weaken. The stone rocked and shook as the man started to regain his own form. The imp was sitting outside the cave just under the stone, when all that rocking and shaking caused it to fall off its ledge right onto the imp's head.

My superheroes and imps never interacted. They never appeared in the same story. I guess I wrote about my superheroes when I felt a need for bravery and courage. By having them save the world, I felt that good would always win out. I wrote about them when I felt good

Activity continued

about some generous deed I had done. If I could do good, how much more could a superhero do? Every noble and fine thought I had, I put in my superhero stories.

I wrote about my imps when I was feeling small and spiteful. When I was mean to my little sister, I thought up imp stories. When I wanted to get even with the kid who made the last open place on the team, leaving me off it, I wrote about imps. When I felt that my parents misunderstood me and were always taking my big brother's side, I wrote about imps. That way I could laugh at my own meanness and get it out of my system.

Today, I write more realistic stories about characters who seem like you or me. But my superheroes and imps taught me a valuable lesson that has helped me create my more realistic characters. I learned that every person has a noble side and a darker side, so my characters are never just all good or all bad. They are a little bit of each. One character may strive to do good, but that doesn't stop a mean, spiteful thought from popping into her mind every now and then. Another character may walk all over others to get ahead, but he also has a deep love of animals and contributes much of his money to an animal shelter. Like people, my characters today are not superheroes or imps. They're both in the same person.

Activity continued

1. Are superheroes and supervillains more powerful or less powerful than regular heroes and villains? How do you know?

   _____

   _____

2. Read the following paragraph from the story:

   > My superheroes and imps never interacted. They never appeared in the same story. I guess I wrote about my superheroes when I felt a need for *bravery* and courage. By having them save the world, I felt that good would always win out. I wrote about them when I felt good about some generous deed I had done. If I could do good, how much more could a superhero do? Every noble and fine thought I had, I put in my superhero stories.

   When does the author feel a need for *bravery*? What does the suffix -*y* mean?

   _____

   _____

3. The interaction between the superhero and the supervillain is what caused fun in my stories.

   Use the meaning of the prefix to define *interaction*. You may use a dictionary to check your answer.

   _____

   _____

Activity continued

4. Read the following sentence:

   There were little mean guys with supernatural powers that they used to misbehave in a big way.

   Look at the word *supernatural*. What is the root. What does it mean? What is the prefix? What does it mean? What does the suffix *-al* mean? Use the word parts to write a definition of your own for this word.

   _____

   _____

   _____

Apply to the Test

Directions: Use the selection you just read to answer questions 1–5.

1. Read the following sentence:

   He liked to look up at that stone and laugh at the **mischief** he had done.

   Which of the situations below describe someone who is up to **mischief**?

   A. a father cooking dinner

   B. a friend knitting a sweater

   C. a police officer giving directions

   D. a little boy playing a prank

Measuring Up® to the Ohio Academic Content Standards

2. Read the follwing sentence:

    They carried people off to **magical** kingdoms from which they could never come back.

    If you go to a **magical** kingdom, where do you go?

    A. to a down-to-earth place

    B. to a place full of magic

    C. to a realistic place

    D. to a sad place

3. Read the following sentence:

    When the Human Torpedo tried to hit a submarine, Ms. Marvel **intercepted** it in its path?

    What is the meaning of the word **intercepted**?

    A. stopped from passing through

    B. let pass through

    C. stopped to talk for awhile

    D. met or crossed at a place

4. If superheroes work **nonstop** to do good, they

    A. work from nine to five.

    B. take very few breaks.

    C. never stop working.

    D. work part of the time.

5. Why did the author like to daydream? Give two details from the selection that support your answer. Write your answer on a separate sheet of paper.

Use Resources to Find Word Meaning

LA-A-F-5.8

There are several resources you can use to determine the meanings and pronunciations of unknown words. Every reference source provides its own special kind of information. Think of each one as a different tool that does a different job.

Here are some sources that can help you.

A **dictionary** lists the words in our language in alphabetical order.

Use a dictionary to
- check a word's meaning;
- find a word's pronunciation;
- see if a word has more than one meaning or part of speech;
- learn where a word comes from (its etymology).

The etymology of a word is usually found at the beginning or the end of an entry. It traces the history of the word.

A **thesaurus** is a book that lists synonyms and antonyms. To use a thesaurus on a computer, highlight the word for which you want to find a synonym or antonym. Then click on Thesaurus. A pop-up window will give you a list of synonyms from which to choose as well as an antonym option.

Use a thesaurus to
- find synonyms, or words that have the same or almost the same meaning;
- find antonyms, or words that have the opposite meaning.

A **glossary** is an alphabetical listing of difficult words and phrases used in a work of nonfiction. Instead of showing all the meanings of a word, it shows how each word or phrase is used in that particular book. A glossary is usually found at the back of a book.

A **footnote** tells about a word you are reading. It appears at the bottom of the page on which the word appears.

A **sidebar** also tells about a word you are reading, but often gives more information. It appears next to where the word is introduced in the article or story.

     Measuring Up® to the Ohio Academic Content Standards

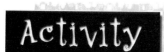
Activity

Directions Read the selection below. Then answer the questions that follow.

Smile! It's Sarah Bear
by Charline Profiri

On her thirteenth birthday, Morrighan Clinco sloshed through crunchy, muddy snow. Then she entered a Russian hospital. "The hospital had dirt floors and dirty walls," she remembers. "I spent most of the day watching others bring cheer to children and adults."

Later that day, Morrighan sat beside a Russian girl. She drew pictures of saguaro cactus.* They were like those that grow in her own hometown—Tucson, Arizona. Without speaking a word, Morrighan and the girl made a connection. They exchanged smiles and shared a friendship.

Clowning for a Cause

What brought this young American to a bedside in Russia? Clowning. When Morrighan was eleven, she attended a camp in Northern California. There, she met Patch Adams. He is a doctor made famous by a 1998 movie. It is about his efforts to bring humor to health care. Dr. Adams taught clowning as a means of connecting with people rather than simply entertaining them.

"He was intriguing, very friendly, and charismatic," Morrighan recalls. He didn't talk down to the kids."

Morrighan learned that Dr. Adams and a group of thirty to forty volunteers made annual clowning trips to Russia. They visited the poor, orphaned, sick, and dying to dispense a special kind of medicine —laughter. Their mission was to make friends and share love.

Clowns on the Road

Morrighan attended the same camp the following summer. She had more conversations with Dr. Adams. When she returned home, she told her parents, "I want to go with Patch on his next trip to Russia." Her parents gave their OK, provided she raise most of the money. Morrighan asked friends, relatives, neighbors, and prominent community members for help. She raised nearly $3,200 for the sixteen-day trip.

Activity continued

Once in Russia, the group of clowns traveled daily to nursing home, orphanages, and hospitals. After a week in Moscow, they took a train to St. Petersburg. "Many people had never seen a clown before," Morrighan says. "We traveled at night so we wouldn't miss a day of clowning. We wore our clown costumes everywhere we went. The only place we weren't allowed to wear them was the Kremlin.*

Sarah Bear

Morrighan's clown character is Sarah Bear. She wears a big red nose, lipstick, and big glasses. The glasses don't have lenses for better eye contact. Morrighan uses a kazoo, a toy accordian, bubbles, or balloons to help bring her joy.

"I've learned to communicate without words," she says. Sometimes she has a translator. But usually Morrighan relies on props, gestures, expressions, or body language to convey her message of love and friendship.

Morrighan spends her days in Russia holding babies and playing with kids. Or having balloon-sword fights with bedridden children. She also spends time with older adults. "I hold hands, hug, and smell balloon flowers with the elderly," she says.

Changing the World

Morrighan misses two weeks of school each November. Making up the schoolwork isn't easy, but she says, "My teachers have been great about giving me extra time and help."

In addition to going to school and clowning, Morrighan volunteers in her community. "Become involved in your neighborhood," she tells other young people. "Give of yourself."

Morrighan's commitment to bringing joy through clowning continues to grow. "I love it," she says. "I receive instant gratification when I make someone smile. Spending two weeks in a clown costume is fun."

---

*__Kremlin:__ This is where the Russian government is located in Moscow.

   Measuring Up® to the Ohio Academic Content Standards

Activity continued

Mahatma Gandhi is a hero in India. He helped free the Indian people from British rule. He did it peacefully. He is called the Father of the Indian Nation.

She has recently returned from her sixth self-financed trip. As long as she has funds she needs, she plans to continue going every November for the rest of her life. After she finishes college, Morrighan hopes to work for Marie's Children International. This is an art program for orphaned children in Moscow. Then she will return to the United States to become a middle-school teacher.

According to Morrighan, the Indian teacher and spiritual leader Mahatma Gandhi said it best: "You must be the change you wish to see in the world."

1. Read the following sentence:

   "He was intriguing, very friendly, and *charismatic*," Morrighan recalls.

   An electronic thesaurus lists the following synonyms for the word *charismatic*. Which synonym in the box best fits the way *charismatic* is used? Use that word in a sentence.

powerful	upbeat	active	influential

   _____

   _____

   _____

Activity continued

2. Read the following sentence from the story:

   Morrighan learned that Dr. Adams and a group of thirty to forty volunteers made *annual* clowning trips to Russia.

   Read the dictionary entry below.

   > **annual** /an yoo al/ *a.* **1)** something that happens once a year. *n.* **2)** a book that is published once a year. **3)** certain kinds of plants that only live for one year, such as marigolds.

   What is the definition of *annual* as used in the sentence above? Name an event that you and your family do *annually*.

   _____

   _____

3. Read the following sentence from the story:

   Sometimes she has a *translator*. But usually Morrighan relies on props, gestures, expressions, or body language to convey her message of love and friendship.

   What does a *translator* do? If you didn't know, how could you find out? What gestures or expressions could Morrighan use to convey her message?

   _____

   _____

   _____

Activity continued

4. Read the following sentence from the story:

   I receive instant *gratification* when I make someone smile.

   An electronic thesaurus lists the following synonyms for the word *gratification*. Which synonym in the box best fits the way *gratification* is used?

relief   enjoyment   satisfaction   delight

   _____

5. What information does the sidebar give about Mahatma Gandhi?

   _____

   _____

Apply to the Test

Directions: Use the selection you just read to answer questions 1–5.

1. Morrighan asked friends, relatives, neighbors, and **prominent** community members for help.

   What is a synonym for **prominent** in the sentence above?

   A. unknown

   B. important

   C. ordinary

   D. unimportant

2. Where did you find out where the Kremlin is in this article

   A. in a sidebar

   B. in the text

   C. in a footnote

   D. in a dictionary entry

3. Read the following sentence from the selection:

   Morrighan's **commitment** to bringing joy through clowning continues to grow.

   Which of the following words could best replace **commitment** in the sentence above?

   A. promise

   B. engagement

   C. pact

   D. arrangement

4. Read the following sentence from the passage:

Her parents gave their OK, provided she **raise** most of the money.

Now read the dictionary definition of **raise**.

raise /rayz/ *v.* **1)** to lift something up, such as a hand. **2)** to collect money for an event or charity. **3)** to take care of children or animals until they grow up. **4)** to bring up an issue or question. *n.* **5)** an increase in salary.

Which of the definitions of **raise** best fits the context?

A. definition 1

B. definition 2

C. definition 3

D. definition 4

5. Do you think Morrighan Clinco will continue to travel to Russia for the rest of her life? Why or why not? Give two details from the selection to support your answer.

_____

_____

LA-A-A-5.1, LA-A-B-5.2, LA-A-C-5.3, LA-A-D-5.4, LA-A-D-5.5, LA-A-E-5.6, LA-A-D-5.7, LA-A-F-5.8

Directions: Read the selection.

Inca Treasure in the Cloud Forest
by Peter Lourie

When I was living in Ecuador in South America, I heard about a lost treasure hidden by the Incas more than four hundred years ago. Seven hundred tons of gold and silver statues and religious symbols lay somewhere in the lonely Andes Mountains. I was fascinated, and I wanted to find out more.

The Llanganates, a mysterious range of mountains, lie between the Andes and the Amazon basin of Brazil. Covered in thick clouds, the trees are dwarfed, and the branches are twisted from lack of sun. The sky is always gray, and the land is saturated in mud. It rains, sleets, or snows often so that a mist hangs above the streams and the rocky slopes of volcanoes.

I was somehow drawn to those strange mountains, but before I journeyed there, I wanted to know more about the history of the Inca treasure.

Early in the sixteenth century, the Inca empire ran 2,000 miles along the spine of the Andes, from Colombia in the north to Chile in the south. In 1527 a civil war divided the empire between two brothers. Each wanted to be king. Finally, Atahualpa defeated his brother Huáscar. He was about to take the throne when the Spaniard Francisco Pizarro and 170 conquistadors landed on the coast of Peru.

Pizarro led his men to the snow-capped Andes to seize the Incas' gold and silver. The long civil war had weakened the Inca Empire, and the Spaniards easily captured Atahualpa.

Atahualpa asked to be set free if he could fill two rooms, one with gold and the other with silver. The Incas valued the precious metals not as money but as religious symbols. Gold represented the "Sweat of the Sun," and silver stood for "Tears of the Moon."

Pizarro agreed to set Atahualpa free if he did as he promised. So Atahualpa sent messengers throughout the Inca empire to bring the gold and silver from the temples of the sun and moon.

Pizarro melted the beautiful objects into ingots to be transported back to Spain by ship, but he did not set Atahualpa free. Instead, Pizarro killed him, and then set out to ransack more Inca temples, unaware that a caravan of 60,000 men was on its way from the northern city of Quito with loads of gold and silver. When the Inca general in command heard of Atahualpa's death, he hid the treasure in the mysterious Llanganates Mountains.

In January 1982, I set off to see the place for myself. After driving all day on narrow mountain roads, I arrived in the tiny village of Triunfo, where I spent the night.

Next morning I hired three men to guide me to the mountain where I had been told the Incan general had buried the treasure. Segundo, the leader of our expedition, was a man of about fifty years—short, agile, and very strong. He loved to smile, and he was accustomed to brisk exercise at high altitudes. But I was not. Segundo was a kind man. He waited for me when I had to stop and rest or when I drank thirstily from an ice-cold stream.

The first day was the most difficult. We climbed from 9,000 to 13,000 feet following the light green water of the stream. At the foot of a high cliff Segundo pointed and said, "Now, Pedro, you must hike up there!"

My heart fell, for I didn't think I could make it. The path shot straight up and was overgrown. The rain had turned the dirt to ankle-deep mud.

"Don't worry," Segundo assured me. "I will help."

I crawled for hours, dragging myself up that cliff with hands and arms. Sharp-edged arrow plants cut my pants and tore gashes in my boots. I struggled to get enough oxygen into my lungs so I could breathe. At 13,500 feet, the air is thin.

Finally at the top, I looked down into the cloud-filled valley. I heard an earthquake rumble far below. We had reached the *paramo*, high flat plains of grass and wet earth called "quaking bogs." The land actually shook when you stepped on it. I felt I was walking on top of the world. It hailed twice and rained constantly, a cold painful

rain. Then the sun came out and turned the mist and streams silver. I was happy I'd come.

After slogging through the bogs for hours, we camped, and Segundo made a fire. The smoke billowed in great clouds, making our eyes water. We all drank tea and ate rice and beans. Then we slept as the wind whistled over the _paramo_.

We rose before dawn. It took us another full day of painful, leg-cramping walking to reach the volcano where the treasure was said to be buried. I was dizzy and nauseated from altitude sickness. I had no idea of the treasure's precise location, and I was so tired I hardly cared about the gold. Segundo only smiled and shrugged his shoulders when I asked him where he thought the Incas had buried it. He said, "I'm telling you, Pedro, the treasure is the beauty of these mountains."

The second day on the volcano it snowed, and the fog came down so thick we could not leave the hut. Segundo said again, "Pedro, the gold is in the magic of the place. Be glad that you are here and that you are safe."

My altitude sickness returned. Then I got pneumonia. Segundo said I must return immediately to a lower altitude. As we made our way down the rocks of the volcano, I heard the roar of a mighty waterfall somewhere. I felt glad I had seen the wonderful land of the lost treasure.

Segundo watched over me closely as we headed back. Coming down that same steep jungle slope to the stream, I realized I'd found a friend in Segundo, himself perhaps a descendant of the very same Incas who had hidden the gold from the conquistadors. I was content not to look for the Inca treasure, for it was not mine. But I will remember the Llanganates Mountains for the rest of my life—that wild, awesome place where even today some say the gold lies safely hidden.

Directions: Use the selection to answer questions 1–8.

1. Read the following sentence from the selection:

    Seven hundred tons of gold and silver statues and religious symbols lay somewhere in the **lonely** Andes Mountains.

    All of the words below are *synonyms* for **lonely** *except*

    A. forlorn

    B. beautiful

    C. lonesome

    D. friendless

2. Read the following sentence from the selection:

    My heart fell, for I didn't think I could make it. The path shot straight up and was overgrown. The rain had turned the dirt to ankle-deep mud.

    The author uses the phrase **my heart fell** to show that Pedro

    A. wants to go back home and continue the journey another time.

    B. is ready to give up because he is tired and weak.

    C. is looking forward to the long journey ahead.

    D. stumbled and fell.

3. Read the following sentence from the selection:

So Atahualpa sent messengers throughout the Inca empire to bring the gold and silver from the **temples** of the sun and moon.

In which sentence does the word **temple** not have the same meaning that it has in the sentence above?

A. At the museum, we saw a restored **temple** from ancient Greece.

B. The headband was so tight, it caused my **temples** to hurt.

C. We visited the ruins of several **temples** in Mexico.

D. The Pantheon is a **temple** that was built in Rome in 27 B.C.

4. Read the following sentence from the selection:

He was about to take the throne when the Spaniard Francisco Pizarro and 170 conquistadors landed on the coast of Peru.

coast /kohst/ *n.* **1)** land that runs along the sea. *v.* **2)** to slide or ride, such as on a sled going down a hill. **3)** to continue moving in a car or boat after power has stopped. **4)** to make progress without having to try very hard.

Which definition of **coast** is used in the sentence above?

A. definition 1

B. definition 2

C. definition 3

D. Definition 4

5. Write your answer to the following question on a separate sheet of paper. Why do you think the author was drawn to the Llanganates Mountains? Give two details from the selection to support your answer.

6. Early in the sixteenth **century**, the Inca Empire ran 2,000 miles along the spine of the Andes, from Columbia in the north to Chile in the south.

   The Latin root **cent** in the word **century** means

   A. ten.

   B one hundred.

   C. twenty.

   D. one thousand.

7. He was about to take the throne when the Spaniard Francisco Pizarro and 170 **conquistators** landed on the coast of Peru.

   An English word based on the same root as **conquistadors** is

   A. conquer.

   B. confine.

   C. quiz.

   D. durable.

8. Read the following sentence from the selection:

   Pizarro melted the beautiful objects into ingots to be transported back to Spain by ship, but he did not set Atahualpa free.

   Which word from this sentence has a prefix that means "across" and a root that means "carry"?

   A. ingots

   B. transported

   C. beautiful

   D. melted

9. The sky is always gray, and the land is **saturated** in mud. It rains, sleets, or snows often so that a mist hangs above the streams and rocky slopes of volcanoes.

   Which synonym has the closest meaning to **saturated**?

   A. moist

   B. wet

   C. soaked

   D. damp

10. Write your answer to the following on a separate sheet of paper.

    Authors write stories for different reasons. Sometimes an author writes to inform. Sometimes to persuade. Other times, an author writes to entertain. What do you think the author's purpose was for writing this selection? Tell whether you think the author was successful in his purpose. Support your answer with details from the story.

Chapter 2 The Reading Process and Comprehension

What's Coming Up?

In this chapter, you will learn how:

- to set a purpose for reading;
- to make predictions;
- to compare and contrast selections;
- to summarize information and use graphic organizers;
- to make inferences and draw conclusions;
- to answer different types of questions;
- to monitor comprehension and ask and answer questions.

The Reading Process

The reading process refers to how you read. It involves what you do before you read, what you do while you read, and what you do after you read. Good readers survey the text before reading and set a purpose. As they read, they monitor their reading and self-correct mistakes. They read actively by carefully thinking about the ideas in the text, by asking and answering questions about the text, by making predictions and inferences, and by drawing conclusions. Good readers analyze and evaluate the text. After reading, they answer different types of questions to demonstrate their comprehension of the meaning of the text.

Text is All Around Us

Reading is important for success in today's world. Wherever you turn, you find material to read and comprehend. You may need to read labels on packages, signs, newspapers, magazines, how-to books, instruction manuals, application forms, and of course poems, novels, and plays.

LA-B-A-5.1, LA-B-A-5.8, LA-B-A-5.10, LA-B-A-5.11, LA-B-B-5.2, LA-B-B-5.3, LA-B-B-5.4, LA-B-B-5.5, LA-B-B-5.6, LA-B-C-5.7, LA-B-D-5.6, LA-B-D-5.8, LA-B-D-5.9

Activity

Directions Keep a record of the different kinds of materials you read on one day. Write each different type of text on the lines below. For example, you might list a textbook, an advertisement, and a magazine article. Compare your responses with your classmates.

_____

_____

_____

_____

_____

_____

_____

_____

_____

_____

_____

_____

_____

_____

Comprehension is the ability to grasp the meaning that an author intended, and then to connect it to your personal knowledge and experience. Meaning is constructed from words, sentences, and larger units of text. The strategies below will help you to read with greater comprehension.

Set a Purpose for Reading

A **purpose** is a reason for reading. Depending on the type of text, you might read for enjoyment, to find out information, to gain a full understanding of a topic, or to locate information.

Make Predictions

You make a **prediction** when you guess what happens next in a story. Make predictions as you read. A good prediction is based on the something that could logically happen in the story. Then read on to see if your prediction was correct.

Compare and Contrast Selections

When you read two selections about the same topic, **compare and contrast** the information. See how they are alike and how they are different. By reading across texts, you can get a much better understanding of the topic.

Summarize Information and Use Graphic Organizers

You can **summarize** what you read to make sure you understand the most important points of the story or article. Write your summary in your own words and include important details from the text. A graphic organizer can help you identify important ideas to include in your summary.

 Make Inferences and Draw Conclusions

As you read, you may have to use story clues and prior knowledge to **make an inference** about a story event or a story character. When you use facts from a story and logical reasoning, then you **draw a conclusion** about an event or story character.

 Answer Different Types of Questions

You can make sure you understand the text by **answering** different types of **questions**. Some questions ask you to recall information that is right there in the text. Some ask you to make inferences. Others ask you to make judgments or evaluations. Read to find answers to your own questions and to questions others ask you.

 Monitor Comprehension and Ask and Answer Questions

Monitor your comprehension as you read. Check your understanding and clarify confusions. Stop and ask your own questions such as *who? what if? where? why? when?* and *how?* to help make sense of a selection.

READING GUIDE

Directions Put your strategies to use as you read. The questions in the margin will guide you.

1 The Wag-o-meter Study
by Suzanne M. Baur

2 I have a puppy named Ginger who likes it when I call her. But sometimes I call her "Gingy" or "GinGin," and sometimes I just say "Puppy." One day I decided to try to figure out which name she likes best.

3 I wanted to be very scientific about discovering her favorite name, so I decided to do a research experiment. Since Ginger wags her tail whenever she's happy, I would use it as a tool. I called it a *wag-o-meter*. I would count the number of wags on the wag-o-meter when I called her by each name and measure how happy she was.

Ginger knows her name, but does she know her nicknames, too? Which name is her favorite? These are the questions I would answer in The Wag-o-meter Study.

The Hypothesis

4 A *hypothesis* is an educated guess about what will happen in an experiment. What did I think would happen in The Wag-o-meter Study? I thought that Ginger would wag her tail most when I said "Ginger," because that's her real name. I thought I would get fewer tail wags from Gingy, GinGin, or Puppy, because they are nicknames, and I don't use her nicknames as often as I use her real name.

The Control Word

5 But what if Ginger just likes hearing my voice? I decided to throw in a *control word* and say it in exactly the same tone of voice as I said her real name and

GUIDED QUESTIONS

1 **Make Predictions**
What do you think this selection will be about?

2 **Purpose** What is a good purpose for reading this article?

3 **Answer Questions**
Who is telling this story?

4 **Answer Questions**
What is a hypothesis? What is the "real" name of the puppy?

5 **Answer Questions**
Why does the narrator decide to use a control word? What does she want to find out?

READING GUIDE

GUIDED QUESTIONS

nicknames. A control word would help me measure other reasons for Ginger's wagging besides the names themselves. I picked "cabbage" to be my control word. Maybe I'd get a few thumps on the wag-o-meter if I called her "Cabbage" just because I would say it as though I was calling her. But there should be fewer wags than when I called her real name or any of her nicknames.

The Data

6 Now I was ready to gather the *data*. Data is information measured in an experiment, in this case, the number of wags on the wag-o-meter.

Ginger was sitting on the floor. I sat down on a chair near her. "Ginger," I said. *Thump thump thump thump thumb thumb* went her tail. Six thumps on the wag-o-meter.

"Gingy," I said, trying to use the same tone of voice. *Thump thump thump thump* went her tail. Four wags.

"GinGin," I said. *Thump thump thump*. Three wags. I guess she doesn't like that name as much.

"Puppy," I said. *Thump thump thump thump thump thump thump thump*. Eight wags! That was even more than her real name. She must really like being called Puppy.

6 **Monitor Comprehension**
Make sure you understand the meaning of *data*. Underline the sentence that defines this word.

READING GUIDE

"Cabbage," I said, careful to use the same tone of voice as when I called her the other names. *Thump thump*. Two wags, that was all.

7 I said all of the words again: her real name, her nicknames, and the word "cabbage," but this time I switched around the order. The wag-o-meter measured the same number of tail wags for each word as the first time.

The Results

8 Almost everything happened as I thought it would. I got six wags for Ginger, which was more than the four wags for Gingy or the three for GinGin. I got only two wags for Cabbage. But that was a silly word I said to see if she would use her wag-o-meter just because she heard my voice.

9 There was one thing I was wrong about. I got eight wags when I called her Puppy. That wasn't her real name. Why did I get eight wags?

The Conclusion

I thought about it for a while. Ginger knows her name, but maybe she doesn't always like to hear her name. Sometimes I say, "Ginger, it's time for your bath," or "Ginger, did you chew up my slippers?"

10 When I call her "Puppy," though, I'm usually holding her and petting her. The only thing I say with this special nickname is "Puppy, I love you." Maybe that's why she likes it best.

GUIDED QUESTIONS

7 **Summarize** Summarize the information under the heading **Data**.

8 **Ask and Answer Questions** What question would you ask yourself to make sure you understood the information in this paragraph? Remember to answer your own question.

9 **Make Inferences** How do you think the narrator felt about the results?

10 **Draw Conclusions** Why do you think the dog wagged her tail the most when she heard Puppy?

LA-B-A-5.1, LA-B-A-5.8, LA-B-A-5.10, LA-B-A-5.11

There are many different reasons why you read. Your reasons should depend on the type of text you are reading. You may read informational text, persuasive text, or literature.

Before you start to read, set a **purpose**. Skim through the text. Take some time to read all the headings or other graphic features, like captions and sidebars. This will help you predict what the text is about and help you set your purpose for reading.

Here are some reasons for reading **informational** texts.

- Find out more information about a specific topic
- Understand a situation or issue
- Solve a problem
- Learn how to do something

Here are some reasons for reading **persuasive** texts.

- Make a decision
- Understand both sides of an issue

Here are some reasons for reading **literary** texts.

- Be entertained
- Gain insight into life
- Appreciate a specific writer's craft
- Enjoy different types of genre

Remember, it is important to set a reading purpose because it affects the strategies you might use to read the text.

For example, if your purpose is to read for enjoyment, then you can **read at a pace** that makes you feel comfortable.

After you determine your purpose, think about the rate at which you should read the text. How quickly or slowly you read depends on your purpose for reading and the difficulty of the text.

If you are reading for information, you may come across words or ideas that are difficult to understand. Then read slowly and carefully. If you are confused, it is helpful to **reread, self-question**, or **take notes**.

If you are reading to locate specific information, you can **skim** and **scan** the text to see if it contains answers to your questions.

You may have more than one purpose for reading. For example, you can read an article for enjoyment as well as to find out information about a topic.

Activity

Directions Read the selection below. Then answer the questions that follow it.

It's a Squawker!
by Andy Boyles

I don't like the screeching of fingernails on a chalkboard. But I can enjoy some squeaks and squawks—if I'm the one making them.

I discovered my love of annoying sounds after I made a simple squawker. You can see how I made it from the picture on this page. I borrowed the ideas from other people, who had borrowed their ideas from others.

Once the gadget was made, I held the cup in one hand. With my other hand, I wet the piece of sponge, used it to grip the string, and then pulled downward gently.

The result was a loud sound that brought in people from other rooms . Some wanted to know who was using a turkey caller, or if a chicken was loose in the building. Most people just wanted me to stop.

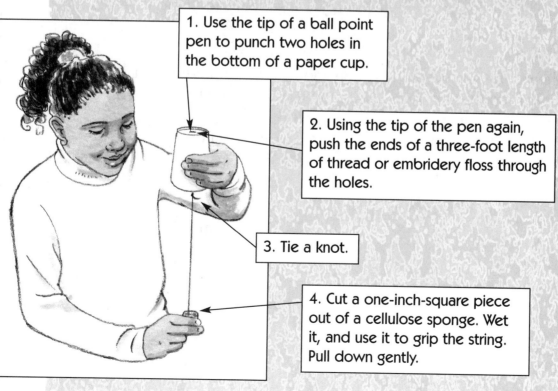

1. Use the tip of a ball point pen to punch two holes in the bottom of a paper cup.

2. Using the tip of the pen again, push the ends of a three-foot length of thread or embridery floss through the holes.

3. Tie a knot.

4. Cut a one-inch-square piece out of a cellulose sponge. Wet it, and use it to grip the string. Pull down gently.

eoples Publishing Group   Chapter 2 • The Reading Process and Comprehension   **73**

Activity continued

I explained that I was learning about sound. "As I pull down, the string slips through the sponge in a jerky way," I said. "That makes the bottom of the cup quickly move up and down, or *vibrate*. And that vibration creates waves in the air, which we call sound."

I looked at my co-workers' faces. Nobody was impressed. "What else can that thing do?" someone said.

I tried different ways of changing the sounds that the squawker could make. I asked my colleague Erin Berger to do the sponge part while I held the cup in one hand and the end of the string in the other.

Erin worked the sponge while I pulled the string tight, and again while I pulled it not-so-tight. (What kinds of sounds do you think it made?)

I cut off the sides of the cup, which made the thing quieter. (Can you guess why that might have happened?)

I thought of other changes to try. How would it sound if I used a bigger cup, or a smaller one, or a plastic one? What if I used a different kind of string?

I hope you'll make at least one squawker to find out. But if you like living in a happy home, you may want to test it outside.

Activity continued

1. Read the title and skim over the article. What is a good purpose for reading this selection?

   _____

   _____

2. What graphic feature included in this article could be used to help set a purpose? Why?

   _____

   _____

   _____

3. Read the paragraph below.

   > I explained that I was learning about sound. "As I pull down, the string slips through the sponge in a jerky way," I said. "That makes the bottom of the cup quickly move up and down, or *vibrate*. And that vibration creates waves in the air, which we call sound."

   How could you make the bottom of the squawker *vibrate*? You have to reread the paragraph above to find the information you need.

   _____

4. Look back at the text. Find several ways that you can change the sound of the squawker.

   _____

   _____

5. Scan the article. Underline the sentence that explains why the writer did this activity.

Activity

Your Amazing Body Clock
by Karen Kawamoto McCoy

Imagine a very special clock, silent and unseen to most. No winding, batteries, or electricity are needed.

Scientists call this special clock a "biological clock." Each of us has one of these mysterious timepieces in our body. Some scientists believe it can be found in our brain. Others believe it is hidden elsewhere in our body.

How important is this "body clock"? Scientists are slowly discovering the many jobs it does for us.

Controlling body temperature is one of its jobs. Did you know that your "normal" temperature rises and falls about two degrees each day? At night, our body clock prepares us for sleep by lowering our temperature. We wouldn't be able to sleep well without this drop in temperature. When we awake in the morning, our body clock raises our temperature. This rise in temperature helps our body to be more active during the day.

This temperature cycle varies from person to person. Some people are early birds. They have fast-rising morning temperatures. Their bodies are ready to work first thing in the morning. Others are night owls with slow-rising morning temperatures. They work better later in the day.

Our body clock also tells us how much sleep we need. Most people your age need about nine hours of sleep each day. But don't fret if you need more or less sleep than that. The amount of sleep needed varies from person to person, too. Just listen to your clock. It will let you know if you are getting enough sleep.

Amazingly, this clock regulates our sense of taste, smell, touch, and hearing, too. Did you know that your senses of taste and smell are strongest between 5:00 and 7:00 P.M.? It's no wonder dinner is the most delicious meal of the day! Our hearing is usually sharpest

Activity [continued]

around three o'clock in the morning. That's why barking dogs or dripping faucets seem noisiest at night! Our sense of touch is just the opposite. We are most sensitive to pain from 10:00 A.M. to 6:00 P.M.

Even food use in our body is controlled by this amazing clock. Take protein for example. It's digested better during the earlier part of the day. For this reason, scientists believe we should eat our largest meal at breakfast. Lunch should be a middle-sized meal, and dinner, our lightest meal. Ironically, this works opposite to our senses of taste and smell!

Our body clock, like a regular clock, must be treated with care. It can become "off" too.

Traveling, especially by airplane, can trick our body clock. Perhaps you have flown from one part of the country to another. You set your watch "back" or "ahead" so that you know what the new time is, but your body doesn't cooperate. It still wants to eat and sleep on your old schedule. Scientists call this condition "jet lag."

You can help your body overcome jet lag by slowly changing your eating and sleeping habits to fit the new time zone. If this is not possible, try to arrive at your destination during the evening. This will allow you to get a good night's sleep. Remember to rest well before starting the trip. Allow at least one day after arrival to rest up. And avoid eating or drinking too much while adjusting to the new time zone. This will only make your jet lag worse.

Even the caffeine in pop can affect your body clock. Caffeine is a powerful stimulant: it increases blood pressure and heart rate. Drinking too much pop can make you nervous during the day or wide-awake at night!

After many years of study, scientists have found that we often act the way we feel. They believe that we can help ourselves by knowing and listening to our body clocks. We usually feel best when we've had plenty of sleep and regular, healthy meals. We feel our worst when we allow our clocks to become "off."

So pay attention to that special clock. It's up to you to keep it running.

Activity continued

1. What purpose did you have for reading this article? Did you achieve your purpose?

_____

_____

2. Scan the beginning of the article until you find the words "biological clock." What is a biological clock?

_____

_____

3. What paragraph would you read if you wanted to find out how much sleep a person your age needs? Look through the article until you find the words "people your age" and a number.

_____

4. Read the paragraph below.

> Amazingly, this clock regulates our sense of taste, smell, touch, and hearing, too. Did you know that your senses of taste and smell are strongest between 5:00 and 7:00 P.M.? It's no wonder dinner is the most delicious meal of the day! Our hearing is usually sharpest around three o'clock in the morning. That's why barking dogs or dripping faucets seem noisiest at night! Our sense of touch is just the opposite. We are most sensitive to pain from 10:00 A.M. to 6:00 P.M.

What senses are strongest between 5:00 and 7:00 P.M.? What sense is strongest around 3:00 A.M.?

_____

_____

Activity continued

5. At what rate would you read this story? Explain.

_____

_____

Apply to the Test

Directions: Use the selection you just read to answer questions 1–5.

1. You can tell that "Your Amazing Body Clock" is informational text because

   A. it tells a good story about your body clock and traveling.

   B. it uses poetic language to describe your body clock.

   C. it persuades you that your body clock is important.

   D. it provides a lot of facts and details about your body clock.

2. According to the information in this article, why does dinner usually taste so good?

   A. The food we eat at dinnertime is tastier than the food we eat at other times of the day.

   B. Our senses of taste and smell are strongest at dinnertime.

   C. Dinner should be the lightest meal of the day.

   D. We eat more protein at dinner that at other meals.

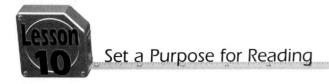

3. Controlling body temperature is one of its jobs. Did you know that your "normal" temperature rises and falls about two degrees each day? At night, our body clock prepares us for sleep by lowering our temperature. We wouldn't be able to sleep well without this drop in temperature. When we awake in the morning, our body clock raises our temperature. This rise in temperature helps our body to be more active during the day.

    How does your body clock prepare you for sleep? You already reread the paragraph above to find the answer.

    A. It increases your sense of sight.

    B. It makes you feel warmer.

    C. It tells you how much sleep you need.

    D. It lowers your body temperature.

4. Which of the following is the BEST purpose for reading this article?

    A. to discover how a body clock is like a mechanical clock

    B. to find information about how your body clock works

    C. to be entertained by an amusing story about clocks

    D. to appreciate a beautiful description of the five senses

5. What are two factors that can throw off your body clock? Use details from the article to support your response.

    _____

    _____

Make Predictions

LA-B-B-5.2

When you **make predictions**, you tell what you think will happen next in a story. Making predictions involves using prior knowledge and story clues to make a decision.

Before you read, look at the title and the first few sentences in a story or article. Look at the illustrations or photographs. Then make a prediction about what will happen in the story.

As you read, pause every so often to guess what might happen next. Then continue reading to see if your prediction was correct. If it was not correct, use any new information you have read to change your prediction. Then continue to read and make new predictions.

Read this paragraph.

> It was a beautiful sunny day when Octavio started his climb up the mountain. High above him he could see the snowcapped peaks. It didn't worry him though as the weather forecasters had predicted clear skies for a while. It was a fantastic climb for the first three hours. Then suddenly the sky filled with dark clouds. Not five minutes later heavy snow started to fall. Octavio was near an old miner's cabin so he rushed inside. Five more hours passed and the snow was piling up high around the cabin.

What do you predict will happen next to Octavio in the story? If you predicted that Octavio would get stuck in the cabin, you made a good prediction. A prediction is based on something that could logically happen in the story.

Activity

Directions Read the following selection. Pause and make predictions about the story characters as you read. Then answer the questions that follow.

The Ghost of Yuckachi Swamp
by Crystal Mandell

Everyone in Yuckachi Swamp knew everything about Donald T. Crocodile.

He loved crunchy crab legs for lunch just like his father. He slithered in the tall saw grass just like his mother. He snarled and snapped and terrified turtles just like his granddaddy.

Everyone knew that Donald did something else, too. He sang!

His family couldn't stand it. "Crocodiles do not sing," said Granddaddy with a scowl.

"But *I* do," Donald replied.

Donald practiced opera after breakfast. He warbled country songs when he woke from his nap. He crooned himself to sleep every night. *Lullabies are so soothing*, he thought. Sometimes he even made up his own song. "Oh la-la dee-dee mee-mee do!" He liked that the best.

Late one morning, just as Donald had finished belting out, "Don't step on my blue suede shoes," Granddaddy covered his ears.

"Enough!" Granddaddy roared. He glared at Donald's father. "Tell your son we need some quiet."

Donald's father sighed. "I guess Granddaddy is right, Donald. You'll have to leave Yuckachi Swamp. Come back home when you are finished with singing."

Donald blinked back real crocodile tears. "Good-bye," he whispered. Then he disappeared into the forest.

At first, Donald enjoyed being alone. He sang whenever he wanted to. He chirped with birds in the trees and crickets in the grass. He vocalized with wolves when they howled in the distance. He even serenaded bullfrogs when the shimmering moon rose high in the sky.

 Measuring Up® to the Ohio Academic Content Standards

Activity continued

No one ever complained. But for Donald, something still wasn't right. "I miss my family and the swamp. I must stop singing," he decided.

So he tried. When Donald felt like singing, he would chew and chomp on big thick sticks. He'd wiggle and wriggle and squirm on his back. He even tried humming. But nothing was as delightful as singing. It was in his blood!

One night, just as Donald had finished his lullaby and almost fallen asleep, he heard a twig snap. He squinted into the darkness. Spooky shadows crept from one gumbo-limbo tree to another. A vulgar voice croaked, "We'll grab all the crocs we can. They'll be perfect for boots, bags, and belts. "We'll become royalty rich!"

"And," another voice added, "We can take some eggs for omelets."

"Poachers!" Donald gasped. "They're heading toward Yuckachi Swamp! My family is in terrible trouble—I have to help."

Donald lumbered after the loathsome men. Suddenly the ground crumbled beneath his feet. He slid into a deep burrow and became trapped!

The men crept closer to Donald's slumbering family. "I have to do something," Donald declared. So he did the only thing he could think of—he sang! "Oh la-la dee-dee mee-mee do!"

Donald's song echoed through the cypress trees, over moss-covered rocks, and along the muddy banks of Yuckachi Swamp.

His family woke up. "Is that Donald?" grumbled Granddaddy. "Why is he singing in the middle of the night?"

When Donald's song reached the ears of the poachers, they halted in their tracks. *Where is that eerie noise coming from?* they wondered. They peered up into the gloomy night sky. They glanced down at the soft spongy ground. They cast their beady eyes from side to side. But they didn't see a thing. "A GHOST!" they shouted.

Shrieking, they crashed and thrashed through the forest and out of the "haunted" Yuckachi Swamp forever.

Activity continued

Donald's family gaped at the trappers running away.

"Donald has saved our family," exclaimed his father.

"Donald, come home!" called his mother.

Donald tried again to crawl out of the hole. Pushing with is strong back legs, he strained and struggled and finally managed to scramble out.

Granddaddy saw him at the edge of the forest. "Thank you, Donald," he said.

"I was glad to help," Donald answered.

"Please stay," his mother said. "We missed you."

"What about my singing?" Donald asked anxiously.

"If you must sing, you must," his father said. "But please sing softly."

Donald felt so glad to be home that he almost sang out loud. But he didn't. Instead he nodded. "I'll sing softly, Dad."

The next morning Donald's father approached him. "Donald, I have a secret to tell you," he said. "Ever since I was a young crocodile just learning to hiss, I have always wanted to sing. But it wasn't a crocodile thing to do. Would you help me with a song?"

Donald couldn't believe it. "Of course, Dad!"

So they disappeared into the forest, far away from the ears of their family. They raised their snouts into the air and warbled Donald's favorite tune, "Oh la-la dee-dee mee-mee do!" over and over again.

Donald yodeled with joy. Now he knew it for sure—singing *was* in his blood!

Measuring Up® to the Ohio Academic Content Standards

Activity continued

1. What does the illustration help you to predict about Donald and the story?

   _____

   _____

2. Did you predict that Donald would be asked to leave the swamp until he finished singing? Why?

   _____

   _____

3. What did you predict Donald would do when he saw the poachers? Was your prediction correct

   _____

4. Read the paragraph below.

   > When Donald's song reached the ears of the poachers, they halted in their tracks. *Where is that eerie noise coming from?* they wondered. They peered up into the gloomy night sky. They glanced down at the soft spongy ground. They cast their beady eyes from side to side. But they didn't see a thing. "A GHOST!" they shouted. Shrieking, they crashed and thrashed through the forest and out of the "haunted" Yuckachi Swamp forever.

   What was your prediction about the poachers? Did you think they would think there was a ghost? Why? Support your answer with clues from the story.

   _____

   _____

Activity continued

5. Do you think that Donald and his father will spend a lot of time singing together? Why or why not?

_____

_____

6. Read the title and the first six lines of this story. What important information do you find out about Donald T. Crocodile?

_____

Activity

Directions Read the following selection. Pause and make predictions about the characters in the story and events that might happen as you read. Then answer the questions that follow.

No More, No Less
A Polish Folk Tale
retold by Marci Stillerman

Many years ago, in the small Polish town of Pinchow, there lived a trader named Leib. He worked hard, but times were bad. He never had enough money to buy presents for his children or a silk dress for his beloved wife, Sonya. Sometimes he couldn't even buy food or wood to burn in the stove to keep them warm.

One bitterly cold winter day, Leib made an important decision. He would leave home for the big city of Kraków. Maybe he could earn more money there. He gave his wife all the money he had and, with a heavy heart, said good-bye to her and his children.

In Kraków, Leib poured all of his energy into his work and had amazing success. After twelve months, he had six hundred zlotys jingling in his purse.

God has been good to me, he thought. I have earned more money in one year than in the whole of my life.

But every day, he missed his family more. He was nearly sick from longing for them. "I cannot go on another day without Sonya and my children," he said and decided to go home. He already had enough money to take care of them for a very long time.

On his way home, Leib stopped in the town of Rozka. He was weary and needed to rest. Fearing there might be robbers in the town, he decided to bury his money before going to the inn. Near a small wooden house that seemed to be deserted, he dug a hole and, looking around to make sure no one saw him, buried his money.

But the house was not deserted. The old man who owned it was watching through his window. When Leib left for the inn, the old man went out and dug it up. He laughed at the stupid stranger who would bury six hundred zlotys in the ground and trust that no one would find it.

Next morning, when Leib went to get his money, it was gone. Tears came to his eyes. "I have never had money to buy presents for my wife and children. Now when I have earned enough to take care of them, am I to have lost it all?"

Looking around sadly, he noticed the nearby house. Whoever lives in that house must have seen me bury the money, Leib thought. But if I accuse him of stealing it, he will call me a liar.

Leib went to the house and knocked on the door.

"Peace be with you," he said to the old man. "I am a stranger here and need advice. The innkeeper told me you are the wisest man in town. Will you help me?"

The old man was flattered. "Tell me what I can do to help you," he said.

Activity continued

"Fearing robbers, I buried my money—six hundred zlotys—in a secret place when I came to your town last night," Leib said. "Now I have received one thousand zlotys in payment of a debt. I left it in my room at the inn while I decide what to do with it for safekeeping. Should I bury it in the same secret place or in another for the greatest safety?"

The old man smiled.

"Since you are a stranger here, it would be best to have all your money in the same place. I advise you to bury it there. Go at night so no one will see you."

"Thank you for your advice," said Leib. "I will do as you suggest."

As soon as Leib was out of sight, the old man took the purse of money he had stolen and hurried to where he'd dug it up the night before.

"If the foolish man comes to his hiding place and doesn't find his money, he'll bury his one thousand zlotys far from here," the greedy man said to himself. "If he finds his money where he left it, he will think it safe to bury the one thousand zlotys in the same place, and I will get all his money."

When darkness fell, Leib went to the hiding place and found all his stolen money. Not a single zloty was missing.

"The old fellow thought he would get more, and now he has less." Leib laughed quietly. "It is no more nor less than he deserved."

On his way home, Leib bought presents for his family. In a few hours' time, he was sitting cozily by the fire at home. His children played with their new toys by the hearth, and his wife looked lovelier than ever in her new silk dress. Leib leaned back in his chair and closed his eyes as a contented smile spread across his face. The kindly trader of Pinchow was happy, and that is exactly what he deserved—no more, no less.

Activity continued

1. How does the title give you a clue as to what the story might be about?

   _____

   _____

2. What was your prediction about Leib? Was your prediction correct?

   _____

   _____

3. Read the paragraph.

   As soon as Leib was out of sight, the old man took the purse of money he had stolen and hurried to where he'd dug it up the night before.

   What was your prediction about the old man? Did you think he would fall for Leib's trick? Why or why not. Support your answer with clues from the story.

   _____

   _____

4. Why would you predict that Leib would buy presents for his wife and children with money he earned?

   _____

   _____

5. Do you think that Leib will ever bury his money again? Why or why not?

   _____

   _____

Lesson 11 — Make Predictions

Directions: Use the selection you just read to answer questions 1–5.

1. In Kraków, Leib poured all of his energy into his work and had amazing success. After twelve months, he had six hundred zlotys jingling in his purse.

   Which of the following is the BEST prediction based on the sentences above?

   A. He will return to his family because he has made enough money.

   B. He will continue to work in Kraków so he can make more money.

   C. He will buy his wife a silk dress.

   D. He will buy presents for his family.

2. "Peace be with you," he said to the old man. "I am a stranger here and need advice. The innkeeper told me you are the wisest man in town. Will you help me?"

   Which detail BEST helps you predict that the old man will give Leib good advice?

   A. The innkeeper recommended him.

   B. He is the wisest man in town.

   C. Leib is a stranger.

   D. Leib asks for help.

3. As soon as Leib was out of sight, the old man took the purse of money he had stolen and hurried to where he'd dug it up the night before.

    Which of the following is the BEST prediction to make after reading the sentence above?

    A. The thief will throw the money away.

    B. The thief will hide the money in a new place.

    C. The thief will rebury the money so Leib will bury the thousand zlotys in the same place.

    D. The old man will wait for Leib to return.

4. When darkness fell, Leib went to the hiding place and found all his stolen money. Not a single zloty was missing.

    Based on the details in the story, what do you predict Leib will do next?

    A. He will return to the old man's house and accuse him of being a thief.

    B. He will return to Kraków to make more money.

    C. He will buy presents for his family and return home.

    D. He will give the old man some money.

5. What words would you use to describe Leib? Choose two words. Then find details in the story that support your choices. Write your answer on a separate sheet of paper.

Compare and Contrast Selections

LA-B-B-5.3

When you read more than one text about the same topic, you can **compare and contrast** the information. When you **compare**, you show how things are alike. When you **contrast**, you show how things are different.

For example, let's say you wanted to learn about the Underground Railroad. You read a magazine article about Harriet Tubman and the Underground Railroad. Then you read a newspaper article about Levi Coffin's role in the Underground Railroad in Ohio. Each text would add to your overall understanding of the topic.

When you read across texts about the same topic, you should do the following:

- Ask yourself how the articles, stories, or passages are alike.

- Ask yourself how they are different.

- Ask yourself if the information in one text supports or contradicts information in the related text.

- Ask yourself what other resources you can use to clarify any differences you may find.

Directions Read the following selection. Then answer the questions that follow it.

Bodacious Bode Miller
by Molly Lowry

Bode (pronounced Bo-Dee) was born in rural New Hampshire near Cannon Mountain. New Hampshire is an important part of this story. There's a lot of snow there in the winter and quite a few mountains! When he was three years old, his mother took him skiing, and he loved it. He especially loved skiing with the ski staff. And the rest, as they say, is history.

The family lived on a 500-acre farm. The cabin in which the family lived did not have running water and electricity because they wanted a simple life. The parents and children worked side by side so

they could be self-sufficient. The parents encouraged their children to be independent and free-spirited. This most likely contributed to Bode's individualistic style of racing. In their early years, Bode and his siblings were home schooled. When he was 13, he went to Carrabassett Valley Academy so he could ski race.

He began competing when he was eleven. Most downhill skiers work on technique first and then speed, but not Bode. All he cared about was speed, speed, speed, and winning. He developed a very original style that was mostly self-taught. It was so original and creative that many people couldn't believe it even worked! Body didn't care, he just kept skiing fast and exactly the way he wanted! Even though people sometimes called him "reckless" or "ragged," the speed paid off.

In 1996, the U.S. Championships were held at Sugarloaf Mountain, not far from his school in Maine. For this race, he decided to use a pair of recreational parabolic skis for the Junior Olympics. (Parabolic skis have an hour-glass shape.) He won the giant slalom and the super-G titles. He did this with a huge 2-second margin. That's a very big margin in the world of ski racing! Everyone noticed this young man. He also earned a place on the U.S. Ski team. He says it's because he wore those skis. Today everyone who races uses parabolic skis! But he was the first!

In 1998, he finished 11th in his first race during the 1998 Olympic season.

Then in 2002, he won a silver medal in the giant slalom. In 2003, he won a gold in the giant slalom. All of this leads us right up to the 2004-2005 World Cup season.

Half way through the season, Bode had a three-month streak of not winning in the World Cup. In eleven of the World Cup races, he didn't even finish. That's what happens sometimes when all you care about is speed, speed, speed! He did, however, win two gold medals at the World Championships in February, but those wins don't count in the World Cup standings.

Activity continued

So as the big World Cup race in Switzerland approached on March 12, 2005, people wondered if Bode Miller could finish. Would he take too many risks? Would he be too reckless? How bodacious would he be? Could he snap his winless streak?

All ski-racing eyes were focused on this race, especially folks in New Hampshire and Maine. This was the last race of the season. Already this season he'd won six of the first ten races. He'd won everything—downhill, super-G, giant slalom and slalom. But remember he'd also had that lack of wins for three months.

Everyone knew that he could have taken a break once in a while during the season, but he didn't. He could have skied more cautiously during the season, but he didn't. He skied exactly the way he wanted to ski. But this was the race that he really, really wanted to win. Why? Because this race is determined by how well the skiers have done during the whole season rather than in just one race. Could Bode pull it off?

Well, here's what happened. On Thursday, March 10, Bode came in second in the downhill. On Friday, he tied with a teammate, Daron Rahlves, for the super-G. He was back to winning! He also came in second again in the giant slalom. By this time, he was ahead by 204 points. All he had to do on Saturday was beat one challenger— Benjamin Raich of Austria. If he could beat Raich, then he'd be the first American to win the overall World Cup title in 22 years.

So how did Bode ski this race—the race that he really wanted to win? He did it his way. He skied fast. He was bold and creative. He went vertical. That means he skied as close to the ground as possible, and he skied down that mountain at 65 miles per hour. He didn't compromise anything and in the end, he achieved his goal. He beat Raich. He became the first American to win the overall World Cup title in 22 years!

Now the big question is whether he'll be part of the U.S. Olympic Team next year. He's made everyone a bit nervous, especially the coaches, about whether he wants to commit to competing. He says

Activity continued

that it's true the Olympics are important, especially if you want mass recognition. But he's not interested in that. He's already proven that he's the best ski racer in the world. What's important, he says, is whether or not he's motivated to race at the Olympics. He's hoping that he will be. In the meantime, one thing is for sure—he's a big inspiration to a lot of kids who want to ski race like Bode Miller.

1. How are Spiridon Louis and Bode Miller alike? How are they different?

_____

_____

_____

2. Compare and contrast the racing style of each athlete.

_____

_____

3. How did reading the first selection help you understand how people must have felt when they saw Bode Miller win the World Cup?

_____

_____

_____

_____

Activity continued

4. Based on facts you know about both athletes, what do you think it takes to become a world champion in a sport? Use details from each selection to support your answer.

_____

_____

_____

_____

_____

5. What other articles about athletes who have independent spirits have your read? Were they similar to Bode Miller or Spiridon Louis? Explain.

_____

_____

_____

Apply to the Test

Directions: Use both selections you just read to answer questions 1–5.

1. Which statement is true about the topic of both articles?

A. The topic is about the Olympics.

B. The topic is about two athletes who won major races in their sports.

C. The topic is about farms and raising animals.

D. The topic is about helping your family.

Measuring Up® to the Ohio Academic Content Standard

2. About which topic do both selections give detailed information?

    A. participating in a major sporting event

    B. Athens, Greece

    C. farming

    D. New Hampshire

3. Based on what you've just read about Spiridon Louis and Bode Miller, which sentence best describes these athletes?

    A. They are not clever athletes.

    B. They are both determined racers.

    C. They are both fearful that they might not win their races.

    D. They are both very cautious athletes.

4. Based on what you have just read, which statement below is NOT true?

    A. They are both outstanding athletes.

    B. They both win major sporting events.

    C. They both grow up in rural areas.

    D. They both pace themselves when they race.

5. How do you think Bode Miller's upbringing prepared him to become the great athlete that he is? Give two details from the selection that support your answer. Write your answer on a separate sheet of paper.

Summarize Information and Use Graphic Organizers

LA-B-B-5.4, LA-B-B-5.6

When you **summarize**, you tell the main ideas and important details in a text. You do not include unimportant details. You can summarize a paragraph, a passage, a fiction story, or nonfiction text.

For example, read this paragraph about fifth grade students.

> Fifth grade students have many responsibilities. They must study different subjects and complete lots of homework. That can take a great deal of time. They must try to get along with all kinds of kids from many different backgrounds. They also have to get along with all the adults at school, from the lunchroom worker to the principal!

How would you summarize the paragraph? You could first look for the main idea or topic sentence or create your own based on what you read. The first sentence of the paragraph states the main idea: "Fifth grade students have many responsibilities." The rest of the paragraph lists details describing these duties. A summary of this paragraph might be:

> A fifth grader's many responsibilities include studying different subjects and getting along with all kinds of kids and adults at school.

A **summary** is a short statement that contains only the most important ideas. Summarizing every time you read is a good strategy because it can help you to understand and remember the information.

At first, you might stop to summarize after every paragraph. Then you should be able to summarize after reading two or three paragraphs, and finally, you can summarize after reading an entire article.

To be sure that you have included all the important details in your summary, check that it answers these questions: Who? What? When? Where? Why? and How? Remember that your summary should be in your own words. Begin with a main idea or topic sentence and include supporting details in order of importance. Do not include your opinions.

Graphic organizers can help you summarize information. You might find it useful to use a main idea and important details chart as you read.

Activity

Directions Read the selection below. Then answer the questions that follow it.

Tree of Plenty
The Coconut Palm
by Bo Flood

Long ago there were no trees on the islands in the Pacific Ocean. No one could even imagine what a tree might be. The people of the Marshall Islands tell this strange but important story about the very first tree that came to the Pacific.

On a tiny atoll called Ailinglapalap, a baby was born. What an ugly baby! Green with no arms and no legs, just two bright eyes, a mouth, and a very round tummy. People came from all across the island—near and far—to see this baby. When they saw it, they stared. Some laughed. Others were afraid and said, "This baby is too strange. Throw it away!"

But the mother said, "Even though this baby looks different, I will take care of it." And she did. The baby grew and grew—greener and rounder. Its eyes became bigger and brighter. How it loved looking all around at its island world! The baby laughed when the wind whistled through the roof thatch. It chirped back at the geckos that zigzagged across the walls. Best of all, this funny little baby loved to listen to its mother chanting words of thanksgiving to the sea and the sky.

The mother sang happy songs to her child, but her heart was sad. Her round, green child had no arms or legs. How would it ever chase sand crabs across the shore, splash in the waves, or swim in the cool, blue sea? When she became old and her child was hungry, who would dig taro or gather fish to fill its round belly? How would her child be happy or have enough to eat?

One day the baby looked up at its mother and made a most peculiar request. "Bury me!"

The mother was so surprised, she nearly dropped her little round child. "I cannot bury you. If I do what you ask, you will die."

Activity continued

"No, Mother. It is time for me to change. Bury me, but still take care of me, and in time, I will take care of you forever."

The mother stared at her strange child and shook her head.

"Bury me near the sea," the child continued, "where I can hear the waves whoosh and the sea breeze blow. The sun will warm me. Bring fresh water to strengthen me. Watch patiently. Soon I will push up through the sand with thin, green arms and reach deep into the earth with long, skinny legs. I will continue to grow and change until I can give back as much as you have given me."

With a heavy heart, the mother did bury her ugly, green child. Every evening she brought cool, fresh water. For many days nothing happened. People laughed and teased, "Foolish mother. Crazy old woman!" Still she continued to care for her child.

One evening something new appeared. Two thin shoots had pushed up through the sand. The mother had never seen such leaves. They looked like the slender flying fish that leap across the waves. She called to her neighbors, "Come and see." They, too, were amazed. They called the leaves *drir-jojo*, meaning "sprouting fish that fly."

The shoots grew rapidly. Soon a slender trunk stretched straight and tall. From the top, branches reached out, clattering in the wind and giving cool shade. After many months, rows of tiny blossoms appeared. From these blossoms, fruit formed— green, ugly, round, and delicious.

The strange child had become the first coconut palm, the most important tree in the tropics. It provides almost everything people need to survive on an island: food, drink, canoes, shelter, and even money!

Coconut palms really do grow as the legend tells. After a "nut" or seed is planted, a thick taproot pushes deep into the earth. Dozens of smaller roots curl down like octopus arms, reaching deeper and deeper. Slender green shoots

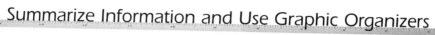
Activity continued

sprout up, and soon a trunk begins to grow straight and tall. Some coconut palms grow to be over eighty feet, taller than a telephone pole. Imagine climbing up, up, up one of these trunks to gather coconuts!

Every part of the coconut palm is useful. Starting from the bottom, the roots are used for fuel, tea, and medicine to soothe tooth- or stomachaches. Roots are also dried and woven into traps to catch fish, crabs, and lobsters.

The trunk of the coconut is utilized for many things. Perhaps the strangest use is saving people's lives. Strong storms called typhoons often blow across the Pacific, with winds over one hundred miles an hour. Parents once lashed their children and themselves to coconut palms so they wouldn't be blown away. During a super typhoon, sometimes everything on a low island is destroyed except the coconut palms. The deep roots of these trees hold on tight. The supple trunks bend rather than break.

Timber from the trunks is used to build homes and schools. The straightest trunks are carved into outrigger canoes. In the Pacific, voyaging canoes still sail hundreds of miles between islands.

From the top of a palm trunk, branches or fronds stick out like a crown of giant feathers. Fronds are used to make mats, skirts, fans, hats, and even thatch for roofs. These broad branches provide cool shade, which is very important to people who live near the equator where the sun shines hot all year. But don't sit right under a coconut palm or you might get bonked on the head by a falling nut!

The most delicious part of the tree is the nut—the coconut. When a coconut palm is about seven years old, it begins to produce fruit. A long, curved stem covered with tiny blossoms sprouts near the top of the tree, just under the fronds. Soon other stems appear. When new flowers begin to bloom, the oldest are already maturing into ripe nuts. A coconut palm continually produces nuts for over thirty years.

The coconut is the largest "nut" in the world. Within this football-sized nut are three very different layers. The outside layer is

Activity continued

a thick husk that protects the seed and makes it buoyant. Coconuts can easily float across the ocean to distant islands. The fibers in the husk are braided into sennit, which is one of the strongest ropes in the world.

The middle layer of the coconut is a round, thin shell. It looks like a little brown face with two eyes and a mouth. No wonder Pacific stories say it was once the face of a baby. Coconut shells cut in half are used as bowls, drinking glasses, or storage containers. Children polish the shells to make toys or hit them together to make music.

The inside layer is the sweet white "meat." The meat inside a brown, ripe nut is hard and crunchy. Delicious! It is often dried to make copra, which is shredded and added to cookies, cereals, cakes, candy, and perhaps best of all, coconut ice cream.

Copra is the "money" part of the tree. The oil in copra is used to make soap, skin creams, candles, cooking oil, and margarine. The Philippine Islands produce most of the world's copra—over two million tons a year.

A young coconut is filled with a clear liquid. Coconut milk has just the right mixture of salts and minerals for someone who is hot and sweaty. When Pacific Islanders sail to distant places, they carry hundreds of "drinking coconuts" in their outrigger canoes.

Legends remind us of important truths. Perhaps this is why the people of the Pacific still tell the story of the first coconut tree, repeating the words of that strange, ugly baby: "Take care of me, and I will take care of you forever."

A Pacific Islands proverb reminds us:
When parents plant a coconut palm,
They give to their children what they need—
Canoes and clothing, food and drink;
A future and a heritage.

Activity continued

1. Read the paragraph below.

> Long ago there were no trees on the islands in the Pacific Ocean. No one could even imagine what a tree might be. The people of the Marshall Islands tell this strange but important story about the very first tree that came to the Pacific.

In your own words, tell the main idea of this paragraph

_____

_____

2. Complete this graphic organizer. The top box of this chart tells a main idea. Add three important details from this article that you could use in a summary.

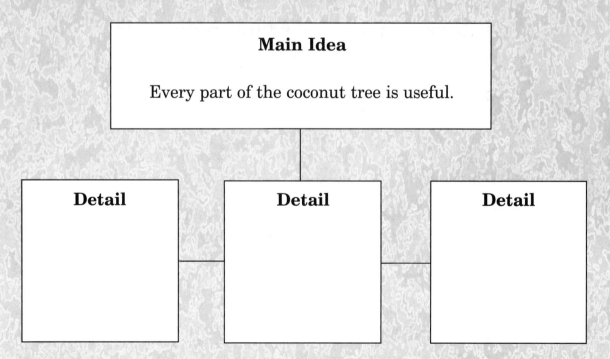

Main Idea

Every part of the coconut tree is useful.

Detail

Detail

Detail

Activity continued

3. Describe copra in your own words.

_____

_____

_____

Apply to the Test

Directions: Use the selection you just read to answer questions 1–5.

1. Which sentence BEST summarizes what happens after a coconut tree turns seven years old?

   A. A long stem of blossoms sprouts under the top fronds.

   B. Coconuts mature as new flowers start to bloom.

   C. For over thirty years, the palm continuously produces coconuts.

   D. The coconut is delicious.

2. Read the summary below of the information about the layers of the coconut.

   The largest "nut" in the world, the coconut, has three different layers. The thick outer layer protects the nut and enables it to float over the ocean.

   Which of the following best completes the summary?

   A. The layer in the middle looks like a face.

   B. Many foods can be made from the inside of the coconut.

   C. The middle layer forms a shell, while the inner layer provides food.

   D. Coconut husk fiber can be braided into sennit.

3. Which of the items below is the best summary of the legend of the coconut?

    A. A green, round baby was born without arms or legs on the island of Ailinglapalap. People said to take good care of it, but the mother insisted on burying her peculiar offspring. The people of the village adopted the child and were rewarded with the first coconut tree.

    B. Long ago there were no trees on the islands of the Pacific Ocean. Then a green, round baby was born without arms or legs. Although people said to throw it away, the baby's mother took care of the curious, laughing baby and worried about its future.

    C. Although people said to throw away a green, round baby that was born without arms or legs, the mother took care of it and worried about its future. After the people of the village buried the baby, it grew into the first coconut tree.

    D. A green, round baby was born without arms or legs on a tiny atoll called Ailinglapalap. Although people said to throw it away, the mother took care of the curious, laughing baby and worried about its future. Reluctantly obeying her child's strange request, she buried and nurtured her baby until it grew into the first coconut tree.

4. Which item below could BEST be used as a summary of the entire article?

A. A Pacific Island legend tells how the first coconut tree was planted. This tree is important to people in the Marshall Islands because it provides them with fuel, food, clothing, housing, medicine, transportation, and even protection.

B. Long ago on one of the Marshall Islands, a mother gave birth to a strange baby that turned into a coconut. This legend explains why people enjoy eating coconuts today.

C. The Marshall Islanders use coconuts for many things. They make canoes from them and use them to build houses. They also use them for food and medicine.

D. The part of the coconut that is worth the most is the copra. There are legends about the origin of copra as well as proverbs.

5. Imagine you are stranded on a deserted island with only coconut palm trees. Tell how you could use parts of the tree to help save your life. Provide at least three details and examples from the article to support your response. Write your response on a separate sheet of paper.

LA-B-B-5.5

When you read a story, an author may not tell you directly everything that takes place or what a character is like or feeling. You may have to use details in a story to figure out some things for yourself. When you **make an inference**, you use story clues and your prior knowledge to make a good guess.

Read the passage.

> Greg yawned and stretched. He had a long day studying and preparing for next day's big exam. He couldn't keep his eyes open anymore. He lay back against the pillows on the couch.

What could you infer about Greg by reading the passage. How was Greg feeling? Was he happy, sorry, or tired? Yes, Greg was tired. You made an **inference** about how a character feels by noticing what the character did.

Story Clues + What I Know = Inference

Remember: When you **make inferences**, ask yourself questions such as these:

- What is the character like?
- Why did the character do that?
- How is the character feeling
- What do I already know about the topic?
- Why did the story turn out as it did?
- Is my inference supported by evidence from the text?

When you read a story, you can **draw conclusions** by using logical reasoning to arrive at a new understanding about a text or story. A **conclusion** is an answer based on facts in a story as well as information you know from your own life.

Read the passage.

> Carla is my best friend. She likes to tell jokes. She always tries to make people laugh when they get too serious. This week she won first prize for the funniest costume in the school parade.

What kind of person is Carla? Yes, she is a funny person. What information helped you draw your conclusion?

Fact 1 + Fact 2 + Fact 3 + What I Know = Conclusion

Remember: When you **draw conclusions**, ask yourself questions such as these:

- What facts did the author provide?
- What do I already know about the topic?
- Does my conclusion make sense?

Directions   Read the following selection. Then answer the questions that follow it.

from **Those Three Bears**
by Ruskin Bond

Most Himalayan villages lie in the valleys, where there are small streams, some farmland, and protection from the biting winds that come through the mountain passes in winter. The houses are usually made of large stones, and have sloping slate roofs so the heavy monsoon rain can run off easily. During the sunny autumn months, the roofs are often covered with pumpkins, left there to ripen in the sun.

One October night, when I was sleeping at a friend's house in a village in these hills, I was awakened by a rumbling and thumping on the roof. I woke my friend and asked him what was happening.

"It's only a bear," he said.

"Is it trying to get in?" I asked.

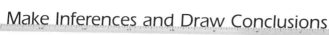
Activity continued

"No. It's after the pumpkins."

A little later, when we looked out a window, we saw a black bear making off through a field, leaving a trail of half-eaten pumpkins.

Face to Face

In winter, when snow covers the higher ranges, the Himalayan bears come to lower altitudes in search of food. Sometimes they forage in fields. And because they are shortsighted and suspicious of anything that moves, they can be dangerous. But, like most wild animals, they avoid humans as much as possible.

Village folk always advise me to run downhill if chased by a bear. They say bears find it easier to run uphill than down. I have yet to be chased by a bear, and will happily skip the experience. But I have seen a few of these mountain bears in India, and they are always fascinating to watch.

Himalayan bears enjoy corn, pumpkins, plums, and apricots. Once, while I was sitting in an oak tree hoping to see a pair of pine martens that lived nearby, I heard the whining grumble of a bear, and presently a small bear ambled into the clearing beneath the tree.

He was little more than a cub, and I was not alarmed. I sat very still, waiting to see what the bear would do.

He put his nose to the ground and sniffed his way along until he came to a large anthill. Here he began huffing and puffing, blowing rapidly in and out of his nostrils so that the dust from the anthill flew in all directions. But the anthill had been deserted, and so, grumbling, the bear made his way up a nearby plum tree. Soon he was perched high in the branches. It was then that he saw me.

The bear at once scrambled several feet higher up the tree and lay flat on a branch. Since it wasn't a very big branch, there was a lot of bear showing on either side. He tucked his head behind another branch. He could no longer see me, so he apparently was satisfied that he was hidden, although he couldn't help grumbling.

Activity continued

Like all bears, this one was full of curiosity. So, slowly, inch by inch, his black snout appeared over the edge of the branch. As soon as he saw me, he drew his head back and hid his face.

He did this several times. I waited until he wasn't looking, then moved some way down my tree. When the bear looked over and saw that I was missing, he was so pleased that he stretched right across to another branch and helped himself to a plum. At that, I couldn't help bursting into laughter.

The startled young bear tumbled out of the tree, dropped through the branches some fifteen feet, and landed with a thump in a pile of dried leaves. He was unhurt, but fled from the clearing, grunting and squealing all the way.

1. Read the paragraph below.

    A little later, when we looked out a window, we saw a black bear making off through a field, leaving a trail of half-eaten pumpkins.

    Why would you infer that the bear came into the village because it was hungry?

    _____

    _____

2. How does Ruskin Bond's friend react when they hear a rumbling and thumping on the roof? Based on this reaction, do you think his friend has encountered bears on the roof before? Explain.

    _____

    _____

    _____

Activity continued

3. Read the paragraph below.

> Most Himalayan villages lie in the valleys, where there are small streams, some farmland, and protection from the biting winds that come through the mountain passes in winter. The houses are usually made of large stones, and have sloping slate roofs so the heavy monsoon rain can run off easily. During the sunny autumn months, the roofs are often covered with pumpkins, left there to ripen in the sun.

Why are many Himalayan villages in valleys instead of on the tops of mountains?

_____

_____

4. Read the paragraph below.

> In winter, when snow covers the higher ranges, the Himalayan bears come to lower altitudes in search of food. Sometimes they forage in fields. And because they are shortsighted and suspicious of anything that moves, they can be dangerous. But, like most wild animals, they avoid humans as much as possible.

Why would being shortsighted and suspicious make a bear dangerous?

_____

_____

Activity continued

5. Read the paragraphs.

> He did this several times. I waited until he wasn't looking, then moved some way down my tree. When the bear looked over and saw that I was missing, he was so pleased that he stretched right across to another branch and helped himself to a plum. At that, I couldn't help bursting into laughter.

> The startled young bear tumbled out of the tree, dropped through the branches some fifteen feet, and landed with a thump in a pile of dried leaves. He was unhurt, but fled from the clearing, grunting and squealing all the way.

What inference can you make about what caused the bear to stumble out of the tree?

_____

_____

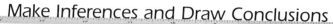

Apply to the Test

Directions: Use the article you just read to answer questions 1–5.

1. Like all bears, this one was full of curiosity. So, slowly, inch by inch, his black snout appeared over the edge of the branch. As soon as he saw me, he drew his head back and hid his face.

   The reader can conclude that the cub inched out because

   A. he was playing hide-and-seek.

   B. he was checking for food.

   C. he was curious.

   D. he was tired.

2. Village folk always advise me to run downhill if chased by a bear. They say bears find it easier to run uphill than down. I have yet to be chased by a bear, and will happily skip the experience. But I have seen a few of these mountain bears in India, and they are always fascinating to watch.

   Draw a conclusion about the author. What do you think he would do if he was ever chased by a bear?

   A. He would climb up into a tree.

   B. He would run downhill.

   C. He would run uphill into the mountains.

   D. He would stand his ground and not move.

3. He put his nose to the ground and sniffed his way along until he came to a large anthill. Here he began huffing and puffing, blowing rapidly in and out of his nostrils so that the dust from the anthill flew in all directions. But the anthill had been deserted, and so, grumbling, the bear made his way up a nearby plum tree. Soon he was perched high in the branches. It was then that he saw me.

    What inference can you make about the bear in the paragraph above?

    A. The bear does not like ants.

    B. The bear was bored.

    C. The bear was looking for food.

    D. The bear had a cold.

4. Which sentence from the article is an example of an inference that the author made?

    A "The bear at once scrambled several feet higher up the tree and lay flat on a branch."

    B. "Since it wasn't a very big branch, there was a lot of bear showing on either side."

    C. "He tucked his head behind another branch."

    D. "He could no longer see me, so he apparently was satisfied that he was hidden, although he couldn't help grumbling."

5. Bears are afraid of people just as people are afraid of bears. Give two examples from the article in which the bear reacted the same way people would if they were near a bear and wanted to avoid a confrontation. Write your answer on a separate sheet of paper.

Answer Different Types of Questions

LA-B-C-5.7

After you read, you demonstrate your understanding of the text by answering different types of questions.

Literal questions ask you to recall information that is right there in the text. If you don't immediately recall the information, you can look back at the selection to find the answer.

Inferential questions ask you to make inferences. The answer to this type of question is not right there in the text. To answer inferential questions, look for story clues from the selection and use your own knowledge and experience to come up with the answer.

Evaluative questions ask you to make a judgment, or form an opinion. To answer this type of question, think about your reaction to information in the selection, an event, or actions of a character. You may be asked if you agree with the author's view on a subject or with what a story character did. You would find evidence from the text to support your judgment.

Directions Read the selection below. Then answer the questions that follow it.

Bird's Nest Soup
by Barbara D. Lopossa

Do your parents give you chicken soup when you have a cold? For centuries, many Europeans and Americans have believed that chicken soup can help cure a cold.

In southeast Asia, on the other hand, people prefer to sip bird's nest soup when they have runny noses and stuffy heads. Bird's nest soup does contain both chicken broth and chicken meat. But tradition says that the soup's healing powers come from a real bird's nest.

Maybe you think, *Yuk! Soup made from a bird's nest would make me feel worse, not better.* But the nests used in making bird's nest soup are not like any nests you've seen.

Bird's nest soup is made from the nest of the tiny swiftlet. Swiftlets live and raise their young in remote caves on islands along the coasts of Vietnam, Singapore, Burma, Malaysia, Indonesia, and Thailand.

Activity continued

Swiftlets weave their nests from long, gooey saliva strands that come from two glands under their tongues. The birds coil the threads of saliva into nests shaped like half a teacup. They attach them high off the ground against the walls of caves. The saliva hardens like quick-drying cement, and holds the nests securely to the almost vertical cave walls.

Harvesting swiftlet nests is dangerous work. Men climb barefoot for hundreds of feet up flimsy bamboo ladders. They carry lighted torches between their teeth. There are no ropes to catch them if they fall. When a collector finds a nest, he reaches for it with a long pole that has a three-pronged fork on the end of it.

In order to protect the swiftlets as much as possible, only empty nests are harvested. When the swiftlets return to the cave and find their nests gone, they will build new ones.

Before the swiftlets' nests can be made into soup, they must be soaked or boiled in water. This separates the strands of saliva from one another. They become like fine noodles. Boiling also makes it easier for workers to pick out and discard feathers and other impurities. The clean, boiled "noodles" can then be used to make bird's nest soup. They can also be used to stuff a chicken or cooked with coconut milk to make a dessert.

Many people are concerned about the continued survival of the swiftlets who bring bird's nest soup to the world. The forests where the birds feed are being cut down at a rapid rate. As the birds disappear, nests are becoming more difficult to find.

Twenty-five years ago, a pound of nests sold for about thirty dollars. Because the nests are rarer now, they can cost one thousand dollars a pound.

A bowl of bird's nest soup costs about fifty dollars in a Hong Kong restaurant. If it really cured colds, it would be worth much more than that. But scientists have their doubts. Researchers at Hong Kong University found that the nests contain a protein that may

     Measuring Up® to the Ohio Academic Content Standard

Activity continued

indeed be beneficial to the human immune system. But the protein dissolves in water, so cleaning nests before putting them into soup destroys the protein.

American scientists are also interested in learning whether soups can help people suffering from colds. They have found that sipping a hot liquid from an open cup helped clear mucus from patients' noses. And they have discovered that chicken broth—as found in chicken and bird's nest soups—does this more effectively than plain hot water.

Even if it doesn't help cure a cold, a bowl of hot soup is comforting and delicious.

1. Read the paragraph below.

> Do your parents give you chicken soup when you have a cold? For centuries, many Europeans and Americans have believed that chicken soup can help cure a cold.

Evaluative Question The author begins the article with a question to peek your interest. Do you think this was an effective technique to use. Why or why not?

_____

_____

2. **Literal Question** How are chicken soup and bird's nest soup alike? What's the difference?

_____

_____

3. **Literal Questions** What is a swiftlet? Where do swiftlets live?

_____

_____

Activity continued

4. **Literal Question** In your own words, tell how a swiftlet makes a nest.

_____

_____

5. Read the paragraph below.

> Harvesting swiftlet nests is dangerous work. Men climb barefoot for hundreds of feet up flimsy bamboo ladders. They carry lighted torches between their teeth. There are no ropes to catch them if they fall. When a collector finds a nest, he reaches for it with a long pole that has a three-pronged fork on the end of it.

Inferential Question What qualities does a person who harvests swiftlet nests need?

_____

_____

6. Read the paragraph below.

> In order to protect the swiftlets as much as possible, only empty nests are harvested. When the swiftlets return to the cave and find their nests gone, they will build new ones.

Inferential Question What might happen if people harvested full nests?

_____

_____

Activity continued

7. Literal Question What are two reasons why the nests must be boiled or soaked?

_____

_____

8. Literal Question How much did a pound of nests cost twenty-five years ago? How much does a pound cost now?

_____

_____

9. Inferential Question If the price continues to rise, what do you think might happen?

_____

_____

10. Evaluative Question Why do you think chicken soup is a good cold remedy?

_____

_____

Directions: Use the selection you just read to answer questions 1–5.

1. What was the author's main purpose for writing this article?

    A. to persuade you to eat bird's nest soup

    B. to convince you that chicken soup cures the common cold

    C. to provide information about chicken soup and bird's nest soup

    D. to entertain you with stories of interesting eating habits

2. Which of these statements is supported by information in the passage?

    A. Bird's nest soup tastes better than chicken soup.

    B. It is easy to harvest swiftlet nests.

    C. The survival of the swiftlet is in danger.

    D. Cleaning nests is harmful to the environment.

3. You can conclude that only empty swiftlet nests are harvested because

    A. people don't want to harm the birds' eggs.

    B. empty nests are lighter than full nests.

    C. a swiftlet will fight to protect its eggs.

    D. a swiftlet will not return to an empty nest.

     Measuring Up® to the Ohio Academic Content Standard

4. Which detail below BEST supports the idea that bird's nest soup may not really cure colds?

   A   The soup costs about fifty dollars.

   B   Cleaning the nests destroys the protein.

   C   Nests are becoming more difficult to find.

   D   Swiftlets coil threads of their saliva into nests.

5. Evaluate this article. Was the information in it well organized and easy to follow? Provide two examples that back up your answer. Write your answer on a separate sheet of paper.

LA-B-D-5.6, LA-B-D-5.8, LA-B-D-5.9

When you monitor your comprehension, you make sure you understand what you are reading. You can self-monitor by using these strategies:

- **Activate Prior Knowledge**

    Prior knowledge is information you already know about a topic. Your own experience, books you have read, movies you have seen—all contribute to your prior knowledge. Think about what you already know about the topic. Then connect this information to what you are reading.

- **Ask Questions**

    Check to make sure you understand what you are reading by asking yourself questions such as the following:

    1. Who is the story about?
    2. When and where does the story take place?
    3. What is happening?
    4. How would I explain this part of the story in my own words?
    5. Did I expect this to happen?
    6. Why did the author write this?

    Asking and answering these questions helps you to better understand the information in the text.

- **Use Graphic Organizers**

    Use graphic organizers to frame questions and record what you learn. Choose a graphic organizer that fits your topic. For example, you could use a **KWL** chart. Before you begin to read, ask yourself what you already **k**now about the topic. Then jot down what you **w**ant to learn about the topic from reading the article. Use the last column to record what you **l**earned about the topic from reading the article. See example below.

What I Already Know	What I Want to Know	What I Learned

- **Make, Revise, and Confirm Predictions**

  When you make predictions, you use clues in the story to predict what will happen next. You can make predictions before you read and while you read. Then you read on to see if you predicted accurately, or to confirm your prediction. If your prediction turns out to be wrong, you revise it based on new evidence.

- **Reread Confusing Passages**

  As you read, you should stop to make sure what you are reading makes sense. If it doesn't, try to figure out why you are confused. Ask questions such as:

  1. Do I understand the meanings of all the words.
  2. Do I need to reread?
  3. What parts of the story are unclear?

- **Check Other Sources**

  For example, imagine that you're reading information about Dayton, Ohio but you don't exactly know where that city is located. Find an atlas with a map of Ohio to help you picture its location. Reference aids such as a dictionary, encyclopedia, or an atlas can help you better understand what you are reading.

- **Use Text Features**

  Photographs, maps, tables, graphs, and illustrations that appear along with the text can help you picture the ideas and details you are reading about. Also, titles and headings in boldface type tell what information is contained in the section of text that follows. Don't forget to check for footnotes that clarify the meaning of unfamiliar terms.

Activity

Directions Skim the article on the next page to get a general idea of what it is about. Then write five **W** and one **H** questions. Look for answers to the questions as you read the article. Then answer the questions that follow it.

5 Ws and H	
Questions	**Answers**
Who?	
What?	
When?	
Where?	
Why?	
How?	

Activity continued

The Hummingbird Trail
by Jennifer Owings Dewey

It reached my ears again, a sound familiar by now, the noise of a hummingbird's wings in flight.

How could such tiny birds inhabit the wilderness I was crossing, a vast lava flow stretching one hundred miles across?

There was the hummingbird, flying fast. Its rapidly beating wings were a blur. Watching it, I tried to imagine its heart. How small that organ must be. The size of a pea? Probably smaller.

I was exploring a region in western New Mexico known as the Malpais (mal-pie). It's a new lava flow by geologic standards, less than a million years old. The landscape is composed of jagged black rocks. These rocks rise in hummocks of sleek, dark boulders, and dip into "bowls" where windblown sand has collected. In these thin layers of soil, desert plants have taken hold—creosote, mesquite, cactus, grasses, sage, and (surprisingly) wildflowers.

The reason for my walk across this hot, dry ground was to follow a section of a trail created a thousand years ago by ancient tribes. They used the trail to travel between two regions that we now call Mexico and the southwestern United States. The trail allowed people to trade with one another.

Cairns, or piles of rock, mark the trail, which is otherwise invisible. There is scant dirt where footprints might help show the way, no soft green grass pressed down by passing feet.

I had felt "lost" already on that first day of my two-day trek. I'd stepped off the trail to sit and eat my lunch, and got turned around. It was a struggle to locate the cairns again.

The hummingbirds were ever-present, like faithful traveling companions.

Activity continued

The wee creatures buzzed and dipped around my head as I walked, iridescent feathers glistening in the sun as if they were made of emeralds or rubies. To me, these little birds lived mysterious lives to begin with, but how on earth could they exist in such a harsh place as the Malpais?

Over and over that first day, I stopped to assess my position, making sure where the trail went. I spent the night in peaceful sleep, tucked into my sleeping bag, having eaten a dry but sustaining supper.

In the morning I opened my eyes to see a pair of hummers inches from my face, so close I made out sharp claws at the ends of slender toes.

"Good morning," I whispered.

The birds hovered in formation, circled each other as if dancing, and vanished in zips and dips over the horizon.

I set off that morning, and right away I lost the trail. How this happened I cannot explain except to say that the cairns, which have the same color as every other rock on the Malpais, suddenly disappeared. I could not find a single one.

I sat down to think through my situation. "Calm yourself," I said aloud. "You have plenty of water. You'll figure this out."

While sitting, I glanced around and took in my immediate surroundings. I noticed hummingbirds flying this way and that in the air, but with an order to their flight, as if they had a road map and were following it.

Watching them, I realized their flights revealed a direction.

I gasped in amazement. I could almost see the ancient people before my eyes, walking on a trail marked by the flight of hummingbirds.

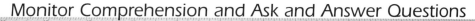
Activity continued

Sure enough, by going east, the direction indicated by the hummingbirds, I soon saw a cairn.

I was relieved, of course, to be back on the trail, but puzzled. How did this work?

As I moved along, hummingbirds dipped and fluttered in the air, lowering themselves to fragile wildflower blossoms, rising again, moving, dipping again.

"That's it, then," I said. The trail took a "logical" course over rough stone, keeping to the low spots, avoiding the heights. In the low places, soil had collected, allowing plants to grow, especially flowers. These delicate "weeds" had a chance here, out of the wind, where water pooled after rain.

The hummingbirds kept near their food source (the flowers), which naturally kept them near the trail.

"Which came first?" I wondered. "The flowers and the hummingbirds, or the people who noticed this and made their trail?

"The flowers and hummingbirds came first," I thought, sure of it. "The people saw how they went, and did the same."

At noon the second day I came to the end of my walk across the Malpais. I sat under a small juniper pine and took a long drink of water from my canteen.

A hummingbird zipped around the tree, which stood about five and a half feet tall. The brilliant little bird dipped once close to my face and was gone.

There is an official name for the trail across the Malpais, which I cannot pronounce or remember. After my trek, I discovered that the locals call it "The Hummingbird Trail."

Activity

1. Think about a land covered with lava, the molten rock that pours out of a volcano. Why do you think it would be unusual to see hummingbirds flying across this land?

   _____

   _____

2. What did you predict would happen when the narrator wrote that she felt lost already on her first day?

   _____

   _____

3. What did you predict about the role the hummingbirds would play in this article? Was your prediction correct?

   _____

   _____

4. Reread the paragraph that begins "While sitting, I glanced around . . . ." What evidence led the narrator to conclude that she should follow the hummingbirds?

   _____

   _____

5. What questions about hummingbirds do you have after reading this article? What sources could you use to find answers to your questions?

   _____

   _____

 Measuring Up® to the Ohio Academic Content Standards

Apply to the Test

Directions: Use the selection you just read to answer questions 1–5.

1. I was exploring a region in western New Mexico known as the Malpais (mal-pie). It's a new lava flow by geologic standards, less than a million years old. The landscape is composed of jagged black rocks. These rocks rise in hummocks of sleek, dark boulders, and dip into "bowls" where windblown sand has collected. In these thin layers of soil, desert plants have taken hold—creosote, mesquite, cactus, grasses, sage, and (surprisingly) wildflowers.

   You can conclude that the Malpais

   A. has lots of water.

   B. is home to buffalo, deer, and bear.

   C. is a harsh environment.

   D. is an easy environment in which to find food.

2. Which statement below BEST helps you predict that the narrator will get lost?

   A. I was exploring a region in western New Mexico known as the Malpais (mal-pie).

   B. The reason for my walk across this hot, dry ground was to follow a section of a trail created a thousand years ago by ancient tribes.

   C. There is scant dirt where footprints might help show the way, no soft grass pressed down by passing feet.

   D. At noon the second day I came to the end of my walk across the Malpais.

3. Based on your own knowledge, who are the ancient traders mentioned in this article?

   A   Mexican citizens

   B. United States citizens

   C. hummingbird hunters

   D. Native Americans

4. Which statement below best helps the reader predict that the hummingbirds will help the narrator find her way?

   A. The hummingbirds were ever-present, like faithful traveling companions.

   B. How could such tiny birds inhabit the wilderness I was crossing, a vast lava flow stretching one hundred miles across?

   C. A hummingbird zipped around the tree, which stood about five and a half feet tall.

   D. The brilliant little bird dipped once close to my face and was gone.

5. How did the hummingbirds help the narrator find her way? Use two details from the article to support your answer.

   _____

   _____

LA-B-A-5.1, LA-B-A-5.8, LA-B-A-5.10, LA-B-A-5.11, LA-B-B-5.2, LA-B-B-5.3, LA-B-B-5.4, LA-B-B-5.5, LA-B-B-5.6, LA-B-C-5.7, LA-B-D-5.6, LA-B-D-5.8, LA-B-D-5.9

Directions: Read the selection.

Bodies in Motion
by Edith H. Fine and Judith P. Josephson

Who would compete in a 50-meter butterfly race, butterflies? Nope. Swimmers.

The 50-meter butterfly is just one of the events in a modern swimming meet. The butterfly stroke is named for the way the swimmer extends and pulls his arms through the water again and again. It looks a little like a butterfly fluttering through the air—with splashing.

Whether you are a competitive swimmer or just a vacation tadpole, learning to swim is smart. It keeps you safe. More than 7,000 people drown each year in this country. Many times this happens because the person never learned to swim well.

Swimming keeps you in great physical shape, too. When you swim, big muscle groups go into action, especially in your arms and legs. But muscles in your wrists, ankles, feet, and neck also get a workout. So do your heart and lungs.

How to Begin

Animals know how to swim instinctively. People aren't so lucky. Learning to swim can take a while. It can take lots of practice to get used to the water, learn to float, and learn to breathe by inhaling with your face out of the water, then exhaling with your face in the water. To build confidence, many swimming instructors have their students hold floating foam kickboards while they practice moving themselves around in the water by kicking. Beginning swimmers also learn how to use their body's natural buoyancy by learning the mushroom float, the star float, and the horizontal float.

Different Strokes

There are four main strokes you'll need to master to be an accomplished swimmer.

- *The Crawl*: This is the most efficient of the swimming strokes if you want to get somewhere in a hurry. It's usually the choice of competitive swimmers in the freestyle event at swim meets. Lifeguards use a modified version when they're swimming out to rescue someone.

- *The Backstroke*: Not the fastest stroke, but nice if you want to check out the weather conditions overhead while you're swimming. It is performed by swinging first one arm and then the other over your head and then pulling each arm back through the water to provide power.

- *The Breaststroke*: One of the easiest strokes to perform, since you can keep your head out of the water for easy breathing. Lifeguards also use this stroke sometimes, since they can keep their heads up to see the person they are swimming toward. In this stroke your hands push forward through the water together. Then they divide and pull back through the water to provide the power.

- *The Butterfly*: This is similar to the breaststroke (in fact, it used to be considered just a variation of the breaststroke), except that instead of pushing your hands forward through the water before bringing them back in a power stroke, you swing them forward above the water. That means less water resistance and more speed.

Safety Tips

Just knowing how to swim well isn't enough to keep you safe. Remember these rules:

- Never swim alone.
- Always swim where a lifeguard is on duty.
- Never run in a pool area.
- Never dive without knowing the depth of the water.
- Don't eat a big meal just before going in the water.

Apply to the Test

Directions: Use the selection to answer questions 1–10.

1. Which of the following is the BEST purpose for reading this article?

    A. to be entertained by an amusing article

    B. to be persuaded to learn how to swim

    C. to find out information about the importance of swimming

    D. to solve the problem of overcoming fear of swimming

2. All of the details below help you predict that this article is about swimming EXCEPT

    A. the title.

    B. the second heading.

    C. the illustrations.

    D. the word *butterfly*.

3. The 50-meter butterfly is just one of the events in a modern swimming meet. The butterfly stroke is named for the way the swimmer extends and pulls his arms through the water again and again. It looks a little like a butterfly fluttering through the air—with splashing.

    When you read this paragraph, the BEST question to ask to monitor your reading is

    A   What is the origin of the word "meet"?

    B. What are some of the other strokes used in events?

    C. Do swimmers play out-of-water sports?

    D. Who invented the butterfly stroke?

4. Whether you are a competitive swimmer or just a vacation tadpole, learning to swim is smart. It keeps you safe. More than 7,000 people drown each year in this country. Many times this happens because the person never learned to swim well.

Swimming keeps you in great physical shape, too. When you swim, big muscle groups go into action, especially in your arms and legs. But muscles in your wrists, ankles, feet, and neck also get a workout. So do your heart and lungs.

Which items below provides the BEST summary of these two paragraphs?

A. Knowing how to swim keeps you safe in the water, and swimming regularly keeps you in good shape.

B. Many people drown each year, and many people are not in good shape.

C. Even vacation tadpoles should know how to swim since swimming is good for you.

D. Some people are competitive swimmers, and some people just like to swim when they are on vacation.

5. Use the Venn diagram below to compare and contrast the breaststroke and the butterfly. Show one way each is different and one way they are the same.

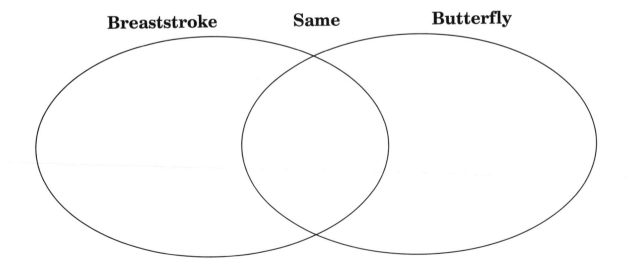

Breaststroke   **Same**   **Butterfly**

6. Animals know how to swim instinctively. People aren't so lucky. Learning to swim can take a while. It can take lots of practice to get used to the water, learn to float, and learn to breathe by inhaling with your face out of the water, then exhaling with your face in the water. To build confidence, many swim instructors have their students hold floating foam kickboards while they practice moving themselves around in the water by kicking. Beginning swimmers also learn how to use their body's natural buoyancy by learning the mushroom float, the star float, and the horizontal float.

Based on the information in this article, you can infer that

A. people become better swimmers than animals.

B. most people aren't very lucky.

C. some people are frightened of the water.

D. it doesn't take long to learn how to swim.

7. *The Crawl:* This is the most efficient of the swimming strokes if you want to get somewhere in a hurry. It's usually the choice of competitive swimmers in the freestyle event at swim meets. Lifeguards use a modified version when they're swimming out to rescue someone.

If you wanted to find out if the crawl really is the most popular stroke in freestyle events, you should check all of the following EXCEPT

A. records of freestyle events

B. a general encyclopedia

C. a swimming instruction book

D. interviews with freestyle swimmers

8. *The Backstroke*: Not the fastest stroke, but nice if you want to check out the weather conditions overhead while you're swimming. It is performed by swinging first one arm and then the other over your head and then pulling each arm back through the water to provide power.

   You can conclude that the backstroke is a good stroke to use if you

   A. are searching for someone in the water.

   B. want to get somewhere quickly.

   C. do not have very strong arms.

   D. don't like holding your breath under water.

9. The purpose of which of the safety tips below is to prevent you from hitting your head on the bottom?

   A. Never swim alone.

   B. Always swim where a lifeguard is on duty.

   C. Never run in a pool area.

   D. Never dive without knowing the depth of the water.

10. On a separate sheet of paper, write a summary of this article. Remember to include the main idea of the complete selection as well as all other important ideas. Leave out unimportant information.

Chapter 3 Literature

eoples Publishing Group

What's Coming Up?

In this chapter, you will learn how to:
- analyze characters;
- analyze plot and conflict;
- analyze setting;
- analyze point of view;
- analyze theme and symbols;
- understand different types of literature;
- understand word choice and mood;
- understand figurative language.

Imagination or Realism

Life is full of stories. Some of them spring from the imaginations of authors. A story may happen in the present, past, or future. These stories are fiction. Fiction contains made-up characters and events. These characters and events may be based on life, but they are still not real. They are the invention of an author. Other stories are real. They tell about real people and actual events. These stories are nonfiction. Nonfiction stories provide information to help you learn about the real world.

Literature Is All Around You!

You can find literature to read in magazines, books, and novels. You can even see literature dramatized on television or in the movies. What stories have you read in school or for your own pleasure? Have you read classic tales, like those in *The Jungle Book* by Rudyard Kipling, that take place in another country a long time ago? Perhaps you have read a novel, like *A Wrinkle in Time* by Madeleine L'Engle, which tells about a family that has a fantastic adventure.

Stories may be told to you in person, on the radio, on audiotape, or even dramatized for television or theater. If you have ever heard a professional storyteller entertain an audience at a festival or fair, you might have laughed and cried and sat at the edge of your seat, depending on what was happening in the story. Then again, you might have experienced a story in a theater production or at home on a video, like James Barrie's classic English tale of *Peter Pan*. What is a favorite story from a television series or a movie you have seen? What is a favorite story you have read?

Activity

Directions Pretend it's your birthday. List five works of literature you would like to receive from friends. They may be novels, collections of short stories or tales, biographies and autobiographies, or collections of poetry, for example. Tell why you would like to receive each one.

Gift List

Title	Reason
1. _____	_____
_____	_____
2. _____	_____
_____	_____
3. _____	_____
_____	_____
4. _____	_____
_____	_____
5. _____	_____
_____	_____

Keys TO Success

LA-D-A-5.1, LA-D-B-5.2, LA-D-C-5.3, LA-D-D-5.4,
LA-D-E-5.5, LA-D-F-5.6, LA-D-G-5.7, LA-D-G-5.8

When you read literature, apply reading strategies to improve your understanding and fluency. Use these strategies to comprehend a broad range of reading materials.

Analyze Characters

The people or animals in fictional stories are **characters**. The author lets you learn about characters through their dialogue—the words they say to one another—and through their actions.

Analyze Plot and Conflict

The plan for what happens in the story is called the **plot**. Usually, the plot involves the main character having to face a problem to be solved. The plot involves a conflict, or struggle. The conflict may involve someone struggling against nature for survival. It may involve two people opposing each other. It may also be a conflict within the character. As you read, you follow the sequence of events that lead up to the solution—or resolution.

Analyze Setting

The **setting** is where and when a story takes place. The place may be realistic or fantastic. An author often includes details to help readers imagine the setting. The setting can have a powerful effect on the characters and on the plot of a story. It can influence the characters and shape their decisions.

Analyze Point of View

The narrator of a story tells a story's **point of view**. Sometimes the narrator is a character in the story. Sometimes the narrator is a storyteller, telling a story about characters and events. When you

read, ask yourself who is telling the story and decide how that affects what you think about the literature.

Analyze Theme and Symbols

Theme is the central meaning of a story or message about life that the author wants to get across to readers. A **symbol** is an object that represents, or stands for, something else—like love, loyalty, war, or friendship. Often, a symbol points to the theme. Sometimes, the theme is clearly stated. More often, you have to add together the details and state the theme for yourself.

Analyze Different Types of Literature

There are many different **types** of literature. They include novels, short stories, folktales and legends, poetry, drama, and autobiographies and biographies. Each type, or form, of literature has special characteristics. Understanding the features of each type of literature can help you better understand it.

Understand Word Choice and Mood

Writers **choose** their **words** with great care. They choose some words, called sensory words, to appeal to the senses. They choose some words to arouse strong feelings. They choose other words to create a special **mood**. When you read, pay attention to the impression, or effect, the words create.

Understand Figurative Language

Figurative language consists of words and phrases that are used in a special way. The words do not mean exactly what they say, but suggest a new and surprising meaning. Figurative language often helps you see things in new and sometimes startling ways. Some common types of figurative language are similes, metaphors, personification, hyperbole, and idioms.

Copying is illegal.   Measuring Up® to the Ohio Academic Content Standards

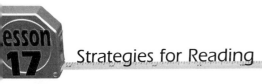

GUIDED QUESTIONS

Directions   Put your strategies to use as you read the story below. The questions in the margin will guide you.

The Great Bunk Bed War
by Lisa Harkrader

1   It started with a wedding. Saturday morning, Howard's mother married Mr. Myron P. Meltzer. Saturday afternoon, Mr. Meltzer moved a set of bunk beds into Howard's room. With the beds came Mr. Meltzer's son, Myron Jr.

"Call me Bruiser," said Myron Jr. "I'm taking the top bunk."

"Let Howard pick first," said Bruiser's father. "Howard, which bed do you want?"

"The top," said Howard.

2   "You'll change your mind," said Bruiser.

Howard arranged his books and flashlight and fishing pole on the shelf of his new headboard.

"Don't get too comfortable," said Bruiser.

3   That night, after their parents tucked Howard and Bruiser into bed, Howard felt a thump.

Wa-lump. Wa-lump.

"Stop kicking my mattress," said Howard.

"Give me the top bunk," said Bruiser.

"Never," said Howard.

Wa-lump, Wa-lump.

4   Howard leaned over and batted Bruiser's feet with his pillow. Bruiser snatched the pillow and stuffed it under the sheets.

"Give it back," said Howard.

"Never," said Bruiser.

1 Plot What event sets the plot in action?

2 Character What impression do you form of Bruiser?

3 Setting Where and when do the events take place?

4 Conflict Explain the conflict.

Howard couldn't sleep without a pillow. He shined his flashlight on the bottom bunk. "I'm going to beam this in your eyes till you give me back my pillow," he said.

Bruiser let out a big, loud, fake snore. *Hoooonkkkkk-SHOOOOOO.*

"You'll go blind," said Howard.

Hoooonkkkkk-SHOOOOOO.

5 Howard tried waiting till Bruiser stopped snoring, but Bruiser didn't stop. Howard turned the flashlight out. Then Bruiser took off his socks and threw them on Howard's bunk.

"Gross!" said Howard.

Hoooonkkkkk-SHOOOOOO, said Bruiser.

Howard tied Bruiser's stinky socks to his fishing line and reeled them out over Bruiser's face.

Bruiser started to snore—*Hoooonkkkkk*—but he sucked the socks into his mouth. "*Ewwwwww*, yuck!" He grabbed the fishing line and wrapped it around the bedpost.

Howard yanked on the line. "Untie it," he said.

"Give me the top bunk," said Bruiser.

"Never," said Howard.

Bruiser unhooked the ladder from the bed. "Guess you won't be going to the bathroom tonight," he said.

Suddenly Howard really, really, *really* had to go to the bathroom. He tried to climb down the end of the bed, but Bruiser poked his feet with a pencil. He tried to somersault over the side, but Bruiser stuck a wad of tape in his hair.

"Let me down," said Howard.

6 "Never," said Bruiser.

5 **Word Choice** Why does the writer use words like **Wa-lump** and **Hoooonkkkkk-SHOOOOOO?**

6 **Plot and Conflict** Which event escalated, or increased, the conflict?

READING GUIDE

Howard tore a sheet of paper from his notebook and hurled spit wads, one after another, at Bruiser.

"Ick!" said Bruiser. "That's disgusting!"

"Yow!" said Bruiser. "Nice shot."

"Whoa!" said Bruiser. "That one almost went up my nostril."

Howard giggled. "Your nostril?"

7 Bruiser started to giggle, too. Then he stopped. "Hey, wait a minute. You shot a spit wad up my nose. That's not funny." He reached up and yanked on Howard's sheets.

Howard pulled back.

Bruiser pulled harder.

Howard flipped off the top bunk and landed on Bruiser's bed. The sheets draped over the side.

Howard blinked. "It's like a little room in here," he said.

"Yeah," said Bruiser. "Like a fort."

"Hey, I've got an idea," said Howard.

He stuck a wad of tape on the end of his fishing line. Howard and Bruiser sat side by side in the bottom-bunk fort and practiced reeling things in.

8 Howard hauled in his alarm clock. Bruiser snared his suitcase. Howard snagged the trash can. It banged against the dresser.

"What's going on in there?" Howard's mother called out.

"Are you boys fighting?" asked Bruiser's father.

Howard looked at Bruiser. Bruiser looked at Howard. They looked at the spit wads and the fort and **9** all the stuff they'd dragged over.

10 "Never," they said.

GUIDED QUESTIONS

7 **Character** Which word tells you that the boys are starting to have fun?

8 **Character** How has the way the boys act toward one another changed?

9 **Plot and Conflict** How is the conflict resolved?

10 **Types of Literature** What type of literature is this?

Analyze Characters

As you read, you should **analyze** the characters in a story to find out what they are like. The most important character is the **main character**.

A writer may describe how a character looks, talks, and feels. **Physical traits** are what the character looks like. **Character traits** tell what characters say and do. Pay attention to how characters speak, move, and act. Notice how the writer describes a character. You can also learn about characters by paying attention to what other characters say about them and how they act toward them.

As you read, notice how a character changes his or her behavior as the **plot** develops. Remember to consider the main problem the character faces and the impact of the **setting** in the story. Analyze whether the character has benefited from events in the story. This often helps you understand the **theme**, or meaning, of the story.

Compare and **contrast** the main character with other characters in the story. See how they are alike and how they are different. How do other characters in the story feel about the main character? This will help you better understand a character's motivation.

Finding out about story characters is like finding out about people in real life. When you meet new people, you listen to what they say about themselves to understand more about them. You also observe what they do and say in order to figure out what they are like. This is the same thing you do when you read. In other words, you add up the details to help you make **inferences** about the characters. You connect what you read about them to what you know from your own life and experience.

Understanding a character in a story helps you to relate to the character, **predict** how that character will behave, and appreciate the character's feelings. Combining all this information will help you to determine the causes for the character's actions.

Authors present characters so that readers can understand them. Sometimes the author tells you directly what characters are like through statements, descriptions, and speech. Other times, the author allows you to make up your own mind about a character by simply describing what this character does and says. For example, the author might give you a clue that Aaron is shy: "When Aaron was with groups of people, he clammed up and didn't speak unless he was spoken to."

Activity

My Korean Name
by Leonard Chang

My grandfather left Korea to live with us in New York when he was almost eighty years old. My parents fixed up the attic so that he had his own room.

He wore traditional Korean clothes: shiny vests with gold buttons, and puffy pants that made his legs look fat even though he was really very skinny. He chewed on small dried fish snacks that smelled up everything. He coughed a lot.

My grandfather spoke only Korean, so I never understood what he was saying. He scared me. I had never seen anyone so old so close.

"Take this tea up to your *halabogee*," my mother told me soon after he had moved in.

"I don't want to," I said.

"He's your grandfather," she scolded. "Be nice to him."

I brought up the steaming cup of tea, hearing him cough once, twice, and again. I peeked around the corner and said, "Here's your tea." He looked up at me, chewing his dried fish snack, and smiled.

He began speaking Korean to me, but I didn't understand him. He waved me over and continued talking.

"What? What? I don't understand Korean," I said. "I never learned."

"*Aigoo*," he said, which was like "Oh my!" in Korean. My mother said that word to me all the time. He waved his finger at me and said, "Korean important. Yes?"

"I guess so," I said, surprised. So he *did* speak a little English.

He smiled and nodded and sipped his tea loudly. He began speaking to me in Korean again. He talked for a long time, and I didn't understand a single word. I said, "Grandpa, I *told* you I can't understand you!"

Activity continued

But he just smiled and nodded and kept on talking. After a while, I just listened. I liked the sound of his raspy voice filling the warm attic.

My mother gave my grandfather a colorful shiny hand fan that he used to keep himself cool during the hot afternoons.

My father gave him a small transistor radio, which my grandfather listened to late at night, tuned to the Korean Gospel station.

My mother also gave him a goat-hair brush, rice paper, an ink stick, and an inkstone to practice his calligraphy, a special kind of writing.

One day I was watching him draw lines on the paper. He looked up and said,

"You." I was surprised. Another English word.

"Me," I said.

He smiled, his face wrinkling.

"You," he said again. "Won Chul."

"Me," I said. "Won Chul is my middle name."

He nodded and dipped his brush in the inkstone, shaking off some of the extra ink. "You," he said. "Won Chul."

"I know my middle name," I said, getting annoyed.

He talked to me in Korean again for a long time, then motioned for me to come closer.

I walked to him. He smelled like mothballs and fish.

He drew some stick figures overlapping each other, swirling his brush easily, quickly. "Won," he said, pointing.

He drew another figure, this time going slowly. The brush made a *swish* sound on the thin rice paper. He pointed to this second figure and said, "Chul." Bringing me nearer so that I could study the picture, he said, "Won Chul. You."

"That's my name?"

He nodded. "Won Chul."

"That looks neat," I said.

Copying is illegal.   Measuring Up® to the Ohio Academic Content Standards

Activity continued

He pushed it toward me.

"For me?" I asked.

"For Won Chul," he said.

My mother later told me that this was *hanja*, a special Korean way of writing using the Chinese alphabet. This was the *hanja* version of my Korean name. She said, "Your grandfather was once a famous artist. All the people in his town wanted him to draw their names."

"Wow," I said, holding the rice paper carefully.

"You know what your name means, don't you?" she said. "It means 'Wise One.' Do you remember?"

"I remember," I said. I held up my Korean name to the light, the paper so thin it glowed.

Not too long after that my grandfather went to a nursing home, and during the next summer he died while I was away at camp. My father turned the attic into a storage room. Now it's filled with dusty boxes of old clothes and shoes and old furniture.

I still have the drawing of my Korean name. My mother had it framed for me, and it hangs in my room right now. I wonder what my grandfather used to tell me those afternoons when he spoke in Korean, going on and on in this strange language that I never learned. Maybe he was telling me stories. Maybe he was telling me about his life in Korea.

Sometimes, if I go up into the attic and listen very carefully, I can almost hear his voice rising and falling, telling me stories I don't understand. I can almost see him in the corner, hunched over, listening to his radio and fanning himself. I can see him swishing his brush over the rice paper, and then pointing to me, telling me my own name.

Activity continued

1. How does Won Chul feel about his grandfather in the beginning of the story?

_____

_____

2. Read the paragraph below.

> I brought up the steaming cup of tea, hearing him cough once, twice, and again. I peeked around the corner and said, "Here's your tea." He looked up at me, chewing his dried fish snack, and smiled.

Why do you think Won Chul's grandfather coughs a lot?

_____

_____

3. Read the paragraph below.

> He smiled and nodded and sipped his tea loudly. He began speaking to me in Korean again. He talked for a long time, and I didn't understand a single word. I said, "Grandpa, I *told* you I can't understand you!"

What do you suppose is the reason for Grandpa insisting on speaking Korean? What do you learn about Won Chul in this paragraph?

_____

_____

_____

Measuring Up® to the Ohio Academic Content Standar

Activity continued

4. Read the paragraph below.

> My father gave him a small transistor radio, which my grandfather listened to late at night, tuned to the Korean Gospel station.

Grandpa often listens to his transistor radio and the Korean gospel station. What does this tell you about him?

_____

_____

5. Won Chul did not get to know his grandpa very well. What do you think Won Chul might do differently now?

_____

_____

_____

Apply to the Test

Directions: Use the selection you just read to answer questions 1–5.

1. You can infer that the reason Won Chul's parents brought grandfather from Korea to New York is because

   A. he wanted to become an artist.

   B. he needed medical attention.

   C. he wanted to visit New York.

   D. he wanted to go to a nursing home.

2. Sometimes, if I go up into the attic and listen very carefully, I can almost hear his voice rising and falling, telling me stories I don't understand. I can almost see him in the corner, hunched over, listening to his radio and fanning himself. I can see him swishing his brush over the rice paper, and then pointing to me, telling me my own name.

   What does Won Chul miss most about his grandfather?

   A. his smell

   B. his artwork

   C. his voice

   D. his style of dressing

3. How does Won Chul feel when he learns the meaning of his name?

    A. He feels proud to be Korean.

    B. He feels sad that his grandfather has passed away.

    C. He feels excited and wants to tell everyone.

    D. He feels like becoming a *hanja* artist.

4. Why is the drawing of Won Chul's name framed and hung up in his room?

    A. It reminds him of how different his culture is compared to his grandfather's.

    B. It is there to inspire him to become an artist like his grandfather.

    C. It helps him to remember how to spell his Korean name.

    D. It reminds him of his grandfather and his heritage.

5. Tell how Won Chul and Grandpa are alike and how they are different. Support your answer with details from the story. Write your answer on a separate sheet of paper.

LA-D-C-5.3

Plot is what happens in a story. It is a series of events that give a story a beginning, middle, and ending. The plot tells what happens to the main character.

Usually the character faces a problem or a **conflict**. The story ends when the problem is solved.

The **sequence of events** is the order in which events happen in a story. Pay attention to what happens first, next, and so on.

Some stories contain more complicated plots that use **flashbacks**. A flashback is when a story starts with an event and then flashes back to earlier events. Stories can also use **flash-forwards**.

The event that lets you know things are about to change is the **turning point** of the story. Usually the events after the turning point lead to the **resolution** of the character's problem (the outcome of the story).

Remember:

The following elements of plot include

- Characters: Who the story is about
- Setting: Where and when the story takes places
- Problem: What the characters have to solve or figure out
- Solution: How the problem is solved

     Measuring Up® to the Ohio Academic Content Standards

Activity Directions Read the selection below. Then answer the questions that follow it.

Run to the River
by Pamela Kuck

"Fire's somewhere close!" cried Margaret as she hurried up the hill to the house, lugging a pail of milk.

There had been no rain for months. The summer sun had parched the land. In her ten years, Margaret had never seen such a dry spell. With things so dry, forest fires were on everyone's mind.

"Mama, I smell smoke," she shouted as she burst into the house, milk sloshing from the pail.

"Margaret, be careful," said Mama, frowning.

Margaret knew that the frown was more from worry than from spilled milk. "When will Papa be home?" she asked.

"He should be here already," said Mama. "I'm beginning to get anxious." Margaret followed her out to the porch.

The air was thick with smoke. Confused birds circled above the barn, and ashes floated down from the sky. Three frightened deer bolted from the woods bordering the farm, heading toward the river.

To the south, the sky was red. No flames could be seen, but the heat was becoming unbearable.

"What shall we do, Mama?" asked Margaret. Her eyes stung from the smoke in the air. Her heart pounded in her chest like deer hooves hitting the ground.

"Wake your two brothers and stay with them," said Mama. "I'll be right back. I must run to the barn and let the animals loose."

Margaret watched Mama race across the field toward the barn. The barn was quite a distance downriver from the house, nearer the woods. Smoke was now swirling in the trees, and flames were shooting up.

Terrified, Margaret ran to the room where her little brothers lay sleeping. Their wet hair stuck to their foreheads.

Activity continued

"Paul . . . Anthony . . . wake up," said Margaret as she shook them. "It isn't safe to sleep. There's a fire, somewhere close."

The boys sat up slowly, rubbing their eyes. Three-year-old Paul whimpered, "I'm too tired," and lay back on his feather mattress.

"Please get up. We must be ready when Mama gets back," said Margaret. She picked up Paul. "Anthony, that's a good boy. Follow me. Hold on to my skirt."

Margaret led them outside. Daylight was fading. The winds had picked up, swirling dust about them. By now she could see flames leaping above the treetops, exploding in the air.

"Mama? Where are you?" shouted Margaret. Suddenly a huge explosion lit up the night sky. Her heart lurched up into her throat, and tears welled in her eyes. Paul and Anthony wailed in panic.

The roar of the fire sounded like cannons as it advanced, igniting the tops of the trees. Sparks scattered in every direction.

"Run to the river!" screamed Margaret, snatching the dish towels that hung drying on the railing. She grabbed her brothers' hands, and they raced through the fields toward the river, away from the advancing flames.

Paul stumbled and fell. Margaret swept him up while Anthony hung on her other arm, clinging until it hurt.

As she ran, she stole a look backward. Dry grass was burning everywhere. Pine needles ignited with the tiniest spark. Then she saw flames engulf the barn. "Mama!" she screamed. But she couldn't stop.

"Run faster! Run to the river!" she shouted.

Activity continued

Finally they reached the water, splashing into it with relief. Margaret quickly bent and soaked the dish towels. She draped one over each of her brothers' heads to protect them from the flying sparks and debris. The winds were violent now, blowing over them like a hurricane.

Tree limbs flew through the sky like fiery spears, and came crashing down into the river. Waves of heat rolled over the water, blistering their skin.

Margaret waded deeper into the river, dragging her brothers behind her. Everything was dark except for the scarlet flames. Heat and smoke were everywhere. She groped until she was neck-deep in the water, holding a brother in each arm, their faces bobbing on the water. She made them splash water over their heads to protect themselves from the intense heat.

Hours passed as they watched the flames consume their land—first the barn, then the house, and finally the woods and fields. Mama's only chance would have been to run downriver behind the barn, away from them.

"Mama!" Margaret shouted desperately. "Mama!"

Her brothers clung to her, dragging her under. It was all she could do to keep her head and theirs above water.

Suddenly she heard a shout from downriver. "Margaret! Paul! Anthony! Are you there?"

"Mama?" yelled Margaret. "Yes, Mama! We're here!"

The Peshtigo Fire

Although this story is fiction, it is based on a real fire.

On the same day as the Great Chicago Fire, October 8, 1871, a fire in northeastern Wisconsin became one of the most disastrous in American history. Because our modern firefighting technology did not exist, the fire took the lives of more than twelve hundred people, and more than a million acres were burned. The entire town of Peshtigo was leveled in a matter of minutes.

Those who managed to get into the Peshtigo River, which flowed through the town, lived to tell of this deadly tragedy.

Activity continued

Mama was splashing toward them through the water, screaming their names.

"My babies!" she cried as she swooped them into her arms. "Thank the Lord you are all safe!" She hugged them and kissed them over and over, wiping off soot with the soggy dish towels, kissing them some more.

Margaret clung to her mother's waist, relief flooding through her.

"Oh, Mama. We were so scared. I saw the barn burning and I thought . . . and I thought that maybe . . ."

"Hush, now, child," said Mama, holding her close. "We are safe, thanks to your quick thinking. I am so proud of you, Margaret. You will make Papa proud, too."

As if in answer to her words a sound came from the shore, rising above the smoke and charred remains, as welcome as rain. Papa was shouting their names.

As she followed Mama out of the muddy, dark river, Margaret's spirits soared. Her family was safe, and they were together.

1. What problem does Margaret face in the beginning of the story?

_____

_____

2. Margaret has to protect her brothers. What else is she worried about? Why?

_____

_____

_____

Activity continued

3. Read the paragraphs below.

> Margaret led them outside. Daylight was fading. The winds had picked up, swirling dust about them. By now she could see flames leaping above the treetops, exploding in the air.
>
> "Mama? Where are you?" shouted Margaret. Suddenly a huge explosion lit up the night sky. Her heart lurched up into her throat, and tears welled in her eyes. Paul and Anthony wailed in panic.
>
> The roar of the fire sounded like cannons as it advanced, igniting the tops of the trees. Sparks scattered in every direction.

What effect do the events in these paragraphs have on the story? What does Margaret tell the boys to do?

_____

_____

_____

_____

4. What is the resolution of this story?

_____

_____

5. How does the story end?

_____

_____

Lesson 19

Analyze Plot and Conflict

Apply to the Test

Directions: Use the selection you just read to answer questions 1–5.

1. What is the cause of the forest fire?

   A. Someone's house is on fire.

   B. It has not rained for several months.

   C. Margaret spilled milk.

   D. The animals in the barn started the fire.

2. Why does the mother leave Margaret alone with the boys?

   A. She goes to look for her husband.

   B. She is frightened of the fire.

   C. She has to let the animals out of the barn.

   D. She wants to get to the river.

3. Why does Margaret leave the house?

   A. The house has caught on fire.

   B. She goes to meet her mom at the barn.

   C. There is an explosion.

   D. Her mom told her to join her at the river.

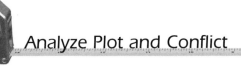

4. Which item below BEST describes the main conflict in this story?

    A. between Margaret and her mother

    B. between Margaret and the fire

    C. between Margaret and her fear

    D. between Margaret and her brothers

5. Explain how Margaret felt while she was alone with her brothers, from the time her mother left until the time her father found them. Write your answer on a separate sheet of paper.

Lesson 20

Analyze Setting

LA-D-B-5.2

The **setting** is where and when a story takes place. Details in the text and picture clues can help the readers figure out a story's location and the time of the story. Use time and place details in the text to visualize the setting as you read.

In fiction, a story setting can vary greatly because it depends on the author's imagination.

A setting could be any place, such as a magical forest, a small town, a country, or an underwater palace. The time of a fiction story can be the past, present, or future.

In nonfiction, a story setting depends on the topic of the story. The time of a nonfiction story can be the past, present, or future. Authors who set stories in a historical period often count on the reader knowing something about that period. For example, if you are reading a story about Julius Caesar, you would know that it is set somewhere in the early Roman Empire, and you may also know that it takes place between 100 and 44 B.C.

A setting can change in different parts of the story. Setting can have a big impact on the characters and events in a story. Knowing the place and time of a story will help you to better understand why characters behave as they do, why events happen, and why problems occur.

Activity

Directions Read the selection below. Then answer the questions that follow it.

Coasting Free
by Janet Plumb Jones

William could see something was wrong as he approached Sherburn's Hill. A group of boys clustered halfway up the slope, their sleds lying forgotten behind them. They just stood there, looking at the snow.

It lay in dirty mounds all over the slope, trampled and flung about wildly. Several piles of ash blackened the hill. William ran the rest of the way, his sled slipping behind him through the new snow.

Activity continued

"Who did this?" shouted William. "Everyone knows this is the best coasting hill in Boston." He set his sled sideways on the slope and trudged to the top. There a jumble of boot prints formed a trail to the old Cook house nearby.

"The British general is staying there, " panted Thomas as he followed William up the hill. "My father saw him move in with all his men."

"Those crazy lobsterbacks think they can do anything they want," complained Nathan, who was as big as a mule and almost as stubborn. "It's not fair!" He grabbed a clump of dirty snow, packed it with his mittened hands, and threw it toward the general's house.

William watched the snowball arc through the cold January air and fall silently into a drift. These were hard times; people talked about war and British ships filled Boston Harbor while soldiers in brick-red uniforms filled the streets. Most people strode about with grim faces and sharp words, but today everything had seemed so soft and bright. Until William had come to Sherburn's Hill. Now a knot grew in his stomach.

William kicked the snow as he glanced back at his sled. His father had given him the wood, a precious item in Boston in 1775, and William had helped cut the pieces and fit them together. Just the night before, he had rubbed two coats of tallow into the graceful wooden runners so they would fly fast and free down Sherburn's Hill.

"We can fight this," said William.

"Fight!" bellowed Nathan. "What are we going to do—beat up a British general?"

"No," said William confidently. "We'll send a delegation. Two should be enough."

"Fine," said Nathan, "you can go. But I'm not waiting around to see if you ever come out again."

"You won't have to. You're coming with me."

A red-coated sentry stood outside the door of the general's rented house. He only glanced at the boys as they approached.

Activity continued

"Please, sir, we'd like to see the general." William tried to keep his voice from shaking.

"General's busy," said the sentry. "Besides, you're too young to enlist."

"We're no lobsterba—" Nathan stopped short as he caught William's sharp glance.

"We don't want to join the army," said William. "We just want to get our coasting hill fixed."

The sentry looked at the boys, then out over the damaged hill. He turned and rapped on the door.

"Two boys here, sir. Say their coasting hill's been ruined."

A-choo! The general's sneeze was so strong, William was sure it would have blown him over if the door had been open. "Send the lads in."

The general sat at a large table, clad in a scarlet coat with a gold epaulet on the shoulder. His long nose was nearly the color of his coat, and he wrestled with a great white handkerchief. The boys' cheeks began to tingle in the sudden warmth.

"Blasted American winters," grumbled the general, stuffing the handkerchief into a waistcoat pocket. "Good day, lads."

"Good day, sir," said William. Nathan just stared.

"I understand you bear a grievance."

William swallowed hard. "Yes sir. Our coasting hill is the best in Boston. We have always used it as a coast, sir, and our fathers before us. In the summer we smooth out the bumps in the ground, and when it snows, everyone is careful not to walk where the sleds run."

The general nodded slowly. He was really listening to William. "Today, sir, we came to use the hill, but it's all trampled and strewn with ashes."

"That would be the servant," said the general. "He cleaned the fireplaces this morning and took the ashes out that door you just came in."

     Measuring Up® to the Ohio Academic Content Standards

Activity continued

"Yes, sir," said William. "We saw the footprints."

"A man's got to dump his ashes."

"Yes, sir," said William. He glanced at Nathan, who was clenching his hands behind his back and turning red.

"But he doesn't have to do it on the town coast," continued the general. "It took courage to come to me, lads. Courage and spirit. You Americans—this notion of liberty must be preached to you in your cradles."

The boys glanced at each other, and Nathan relaxed.

"Captain!" called the general.

A soldier entered from the hall and gave a crisp salute. "Sir."

"Appoint a detail to repair the coasting hill out front."

"Yes, sir."

"And bring some more tea—steaming hot."

Three soldiers armed with shovels followed William and Nathan through the glistening snow. Thomas and the other boys sat on their sleds, watching with open mouths.

"Come on," William shouted to them. "Let's all help."

An hour later William stood at the top of the hill, holding his new sled. Then he flopped onto the smooth wood and flew down Sherburn's Hill, the wind whistling in his ears. He had never felt so free.

1. Where and when does the story take place?

    _____

2. What details indicate the historical period of this story?

    _____

    _____

    _____

Activity continued

3. At the beginning of the story, how is the snow different from the way it usually is? What does this difference suggest to the boys?

_____

_____

4. What about the words used by the general and William gives the story a flavor of the historical period in which it is set?

_____

_____

5. Why does William decide to help the soldiers? What effect does this have on the story's conclusion?

_____

_____

_____

Apply to the Test

Directions: Use both selections you just read to answer questions 1–5.

1. How does the author emphasize how the setting disturbs the boys in the opening of the story?

   A. She suggests that the Revolutionary War is about to happen.

   B. She contrasts the black ash with the new snow.

   C. She shows William running to Sherburn's Hill with his sled.

   D. She describes the boys' forgotten sleds.

2. Which detail below does NOT support the idea that times were harder now in Boston than they were in the past?

    A. There is talk of war.

    B. There are many British soldiers on the street.

    C. It is a cold January.

    D. Ships with British soldiers fill the harbor.

3. The description of the atmosphere in the general's house

    A. adds to the threatening quality of the general.

    B. shows the military discipline of the British.

    C. shows how the British tried to impress Americans.

    D. makes the general seem less threatening.

4. Which statement from the story indicates that the British general understands the American spirit?

    A. "He cleaned the fireplaces this morning and took the ashes out that door you just came in."

    B. "You Americans—this notion of liberty must be preached to you in your cradles."

    C. "I understand you have a grievance."

    D. "A man's got to dump his ashes."

5. Explain why at the end of the story, William "never felt so free." Include details from the story to support your answer. Write your answer on a separate sheet of paper.

Point of view is the vantage point or angle from which a story is told. A story can be told from three different points of view: **first person, third person omniscient**, and **third person limited**.

Sometimes a story is told from the **first-person point of view**. One character in the story tells about the other characters and the events. This character, who is the **narrator**, is identified by the pronoun *I*. When you read a story told in the first person, you see the world through the narrator's eyes. Sometimes, you may find that you don't agree with something the narrator says, but you have to depend on him or her for the information you get about everything.

Here is an example of a story told in the first person. Notice that you find out things about the narrator that only he knows.

> Today was the last math class of the year, and was I glad! Just because I make good grades in math, everybody calls me the "Number Whiz." Mr. Thompson, the math teacher, is always using my solutions to show the class how to solve problems. I can't tell him or anybody else how much I hate math. Yes, I'm good at it, and I really need the grade points. The math problems that cause other kids to sweat and worry are easy for me. I guess just because you're good at something doesn't mean you like it.

Sometimes a story is told in the third person. All the characters are identified by the pronouns *he* or *she*. The narrator stands outside the story and seems to know everything about all the characters and events. This narrator can tell what everybody is thinking and what is happening everywhere. This is called the **third person omniscient point of view**. (Omniscient, pronounced om•nish•ent, means "all-knowing.")

For example, the narrator might tell you about a character's family in a story.

> The Henderson family had lived near the big racetrack at Saratoga for as long as anyone could remember. But they had never been interested in horse racing. Old Man Henderson thought that horses were a thing of the past. He saw cars and tractors as more useful. And if something wasn't useful, what worth could it have? His son Jared had different ideas. Jared imagined himself owning a stable with beautiful, fast horses. He had dreams of big parties on wide lawns with wealthy friends. He saw himself traveling to racetracks around the world. This would have surprised his mother. She couldn't wait to get away from horses and everything about them to live by the sea.

Sometimes a story is told in the third person, but it focuses on one specific character. The narrator shares the feelings and thoughts of that character only. This is the **third-person limited point of view**.

For example, in the paragraph below, notice how the narrator focuses on one character—Rosalie. You learn what Rosalie is thinking.

> Rosalie was upset. She wanted Daria to like her. But Daria didn't pay much attention to her. She hated the way that Daria sort of flipped her hair when she talked to her. She seemed to be looking around for someone else to talk to. She should be paying attention to what I'm saying, Rosalie thought. Just to get her attention, Rosalie decided to say something really shocking. "There's a huge bug crawling up your sock, Daria," she shouted. But Daria was already walking away toward Jenna, the most popular girl in school. She makes me feels like I'm invisible, Rosalie thought.

Activity **Directions** Read the following selection. Then answer the questions that follow it.

Swimming Lesson
by John Moir

The lone sailboat bounced across the choppy water, racing for the darkening, pine-covered shore more than mile away. Katie shivered as she scanned the black clouds billowing over the mountains. She glanced at her older brother, Rick. "You think we have enough time?"

"Of course, of course," said Rick, pushing back his tangled blond hair. "Only a few more minutes, then you can impress everyone tonight with your tales of adventure on the high seas of Lake Tahoe." His voice barely carried over the wind.

The boat lurched heavily, and Rick's half-eaten sandwich slid off the seat beside him to the deck of the boat's cockpit. He ignored it, using both hands to steady the tiller. Above them, the straining sail emitted an uneven hum.

"Just get us back before the storm hits," shouted Katie. She fastened her windbreaker under her life jacket as a peal of thunder rolled across the water. The shore still looked much too far away.

She wished she'd voiced her doubts earlier when Rick had casually dismissed the threat of a storm. But Katie was only in sixth grade, and sixteen-year-old Rich wasn't about to listen to her.

"At least you're on the swim team." Rick flashed a quick smile. "In case we need to swim."

Katie had a new swim coach this year, a soft-spoken man named Mr. Fleet. Katie soon discovered that he had some strange notions. She remembered the first workout of the season, when Mr. Fleet insisted that the team jump into the pool again and again, trying to enter the water without a splash. He said that gracefulness in the water, letting the water help you, was the key to success.

A powerful gust of wind tipped the boat's mast dangerously close to the water.

"Hold the tiller," Rick yelled, "while I take in some sail."

Measuring Up® to the Ohio Academic Content Standard

Activity continued

The tiller's taped handle, rough on Katie's palms, bucked and jerked. Rick took a tentative stop as the boat pitched sharply. He managed to move another step while grabbing for a handhold. Suddenly a huge gust of wind roared over the boat and tore the tiller from Katie's hands. Katie stared helplessly at Rick as the boat swung into the wind, the sail flapping uselessly.

"Just sit tight," Rick yelled. "I'll be right there!"

Drops of rain began to pelt the deck. Another violent gust of wind roared over the boat, throwing Katie off-balance and splintering the mast near the base with a sharp crack.

Katie pitched backward into the icy lake. As the cold closed around her, she saw the broken mast and sail collapsing toward her head. She was thrown deep into the water. Then her life jacket pulled her up into a tangled mass of lines and sail that blocked her way to the surface. Stunned by the sudden dunking, Katie floated just below the surface, clawing feebly at the fabric of the sail that trapped her.

A great tiredness settled over her, and her thoughts drifted to the warm, aqua-blue water of the swimming pool where her team practiced. Katie saw an image of Mr. Fleet with his watchful eyes and confident, fluid movements.

She punched at the fabric above her head as the cold drained her energy, She knew she had to act quickly. The weariness in her body grew heavier.

The image of the swimming pool returned. *Relax with the water. Let the water help you.* Mr. Fleet's calm words echoed in her mind.

Katie grabbed again at the sail above her and pushed hard, but this only forced her down into the water until her life jacket pulled her up again. The sail remained like a sheet of ice, trapping her.

Above her and to the right Katie saw a small patch of water opening and closing as the wreckage shifted. She struggled toward the opening, her lungs feeling as if they would burst. She was just inches away when her windbreaker snagged on a line. She couldn't move.

Activity continued

Relax with the water. Mr. Fleet's words were unhurried, comforting. *All right, all right!* thought Katie. Forcing herself to relax, she allowed her body to drift while she worked to free the line. With her last bit of energy, she broke loose and thrust her head up through the opening.

It was the sweetest breath of her life.

"Katie? Katie?" Somewhere Rick was calling. Katie saw the boat, stable in the water, with the mast and sail a great tangled mess dragging off the side.

"Katie, over here!" Rick stood on the deck looking down at her, gesturing wildly. Katie dog-paddled to the hull of the boat. "You OK? I couldn't see you in the water." Rick's face looked thin and drained of color. "You were down there a long time. A long time."

"I'm OK," Katie said.

"I really messed up," Rick said in a subdued voice.

The rain was easing off a bit, and the clouds arching across the sky reverberated with color. *I'm alive!* Katie thought. All at once she was filled with energy.

"Thanks Mr. Fleet," she said softly. "Thanks."

     Measuring Up® to the Ohio Academic Content Standards

Activity continued

1. How do you know that this selection is written in the third person?

   _____

   _____

   _____

2. Read the paragraph below.

   > The lone sailboat bounced across the choppy water, racing for the darkening, pine-covered shore more than mile away. Katie shivered as she scanned the black clouds billowing over the mountains. She glanced at her older brother, Rick. "You think we have enough time?"

   How do you know that the sailboat Katie and Rick are in is the only one on the lake?

   _____

   _____

   _____

3. Read the paragraph below.

   > She wished she'd voiced her doubts earlier when Rick had casually dismissed the threat of a storm. But Katie was only in sixth grade, and sixteen-year-old Rich wasn't about to listen to her.

   Why does Katie think that Rick doesn't pay attention to what she says, according to the narrator?

   _____

   _____

   _____

Activity continued

4. Read the paragraph below

    Katie had a new swim coach this year, a soft-spoken man named Mr. Fleet. Katie soon discovered that he had some strange notions. She remembered the first workout of the season, when Mr. Fleet insisted that the team jump into the pool again and again, trying to enter the water without a splash. He said that gracefulness in the water, letting the water help you was the key to success.

    What did Katie learn from Mr. Fleet, her swimming coach?

    _____

    _____

    _____

5. How does the narrator take you inside Katie's mind when she is in the water?

    _____

    _____

    _____

Directions: Use the selection you just read to answer questions 1–5.

1. She wished she'd voiced her doubts earlier when Rick had casually dismissed the threat of a storm.

    If this story were told in the first person from Katie's point of view, how would this sentence be written?

    A. Katie wished she'd voiced her doubts earlier when Rick had casually dismissed the threat of a storm.

    B. I wished I'd voiced my doubts earlier when Rick had casually dismissed the threat of a storm.

    C. You could have voiced your doubts earlier, she thought, when Rick had casually dismissed the threat of a storm.

    D. Her doubts could have been voiced earlier when Rick had casually dismissed the threat of a storm.

2. A great tiredness settled over her, and her thoughts drifted to the warm, aqua-blue water of the swimming pool where her team practiced. Katie saw an image of Mr. Fleet with his watchful eyes and confident, fluid movements.

    How do you know that Katie will try not to give up in the water?

    A. She is so exhausted but feels a new surge of power.

    B. She wants to go back to the warm waters of the pool.

    C. She is thinking about the lesson she learned from Mr. Fleet.

    D. She realizes that she wants to see Mr. Fleet again.

3. Throughout the story, the narrator suggests the fear in Katie's mind by

   A. describing her feeling of panic.

   B. describing the sail as a sheet of ice.

   C. observing how her life jacket works.

   D. hinting at a possible rescue.

4. Katie's thoughts of Mr. Fleet

   A display hero-worship.

   B. are like a private conversation.

   C. show her contempt for Rick.

   D. suggest that Katie might drown.

5. Explain what the narrator means when he says "it was the sweetest breath of Katie's life?" Be sure to include two details from the passage to support your answer. Write your answer on a separate sheet of paper.

   Measuring Up® to the Ohio Academic Content Standard

LA-D-E-5.5

Theme is the insight into life you gain from reading a story. It is the overall idea, or message about life, that the author wants to convey to readers. Sometimes the theme of a story is stated clearly by the author. Most of the time, however, the theme is not immediately clear. By discovering the theme of a story, you will understand what the author thinks or feels is important and meaningful.

A **symbol** is an object used to represent ideas. For example, the author might use a dove to stand for peace or a mirror to stand for vanity. Interpreting symbols can help you understand the theme.

To identify the theme, you should

- think about what the characters do and say;
- think about what happens as a result of characters' words and actions;
- think about what message the author wants to get across.

Themes can usually be expressed as one or two sentences about life or people in general. For example: A good friendship is worth a lot of patience and tolerance.

Some themes are **universal**. This means that they span different times and cultures. You might find the same theme about friendship in a folktale from Africa and in a short story from Japan. You might even find the same theme in a movie you see on television.

In order to infer the theme of a selection, you have to keep in mind the other elements of fiction: plot, characters, and setting. Everything in a story contributes in some way to a story's theme.

Activity

Directions Read the selection below. Then answer the questions that follow it.

Will Power
by Kimberly Brubaker Bradley

Caitlin sat in the moving car and tried to imagine the color blue. Light blue, shining and deep, like the clear water of a swimming pool. Caitlin tried hard. She knew she should be able to remember what things looked like. She had only been blind for two months, and she had been able to see for twelve years. In her mind she could picture the green of the hills around her home. She could imagine her baby sister's dark brown hair. But light blue, perfect water-blue, always eluded her.

"Here we are," her mother said. "We're at the pool." Today was the first day since her parents' van had overturned on the highway that Caitlin was allowed to get back in the water. The doctors said her skull fracture had healed. Her eyes would never heal. She would never see again.

Caitlin opened the car door and waited for her mother to come get her. She held her mother's arm while they climbed the steps to the pool entrance. In the locker room she could hear whispers from the other girls.

"She was the best junior swimmer in the country."

"Everyone said she would be in the Olympics for sure."

Caitlin pretended she didn't hear. The Olympics were all she'd dreamed about. At the last Junior Nationals she'd won five gold medals. She had planned to move up to the Seniors this year—until the van skidded out of control.

"Hey, Caitie!" A sudden touch on her shoulder made her jump. "Sorry," the voice said awkwardly.

"It's OK," Caitlin said. "You just startled me."

"It's Jenny," the voice said.

I know. I recognized you."

Activity continued

Jenny was the second-best swimmer on the Junior team. She swam breaststroke faster than Caitlin. Now, Caitlin realized, Jenny swam everything faster.

"I just wanted to say good luck," Jenny said.

"Thanks." Caitlin wondered why no one else had spoken to her. She and Jenny had never been close friends.

She got into the water slowly. It lapped around her, cold and inviting. She pushed off slowly and began to swim.

Three strokes later, she hit the lane marker. She corrected her course and stroked out again. She hit the marker on the other side. She floundered and clutched the lane marker, sputtering.

She stroked out again. Hit the marker. Again. She switched to breaststroke, her least-favorite stroke. Without warning, she hit the wall hard.

Caitlin persevered. She swam six laps. They were the slowest six laps of her life. Her legs trembled from exhaustion, and her hand was swollen from banging it into the end of the pool. All around her she heard waves slapping, people shouting, her coach whistling.

She didn't belong here anymore.

She got out of the pool and stood until her mother came to help her. "It's only your first day, Caitie," her mother said.

Caitlin shook her head. "I can't do this."

After that, Caitlin stayed at home. She took physical therapy and started learning how to be independent without her vision. She learned to walk with a white cane and to read Braille. In the fall she would return to school.

She would not return to the pool. She still could not remember the color blue. She stopped trying.

Her old coach brought her a brochure on the Paralympics. He read it out loud to her. She could swim against serious athletes who were blind or physically challenged. When he left, Caitlin thought for a long time.

 Chapter 3 • Literature **177**

Activity continued

After getting her mom's OK, she took her cane and walked to the bus stop on the corner. When the bus came, she asked the driver to tell her the stops. She arrived at the pool.

The girls' locker room was empty, but Caitlin heard voices coming from the pool. She found a bench by the side of the pool and sat down. The warm smell of chlorine enveloped her. When practice was over, she asked someone to find Jenny for her.

"Hi, Caitlin. What's up?" Jenny sat next to her. Caitlin could hear her wiping her face with a towel.

Caitlin explained her problem. "I need help from someone who can read."

"No problem." Caitlin thought she could hear Jenny smile.

They took another bus to the library. Caitlin held Jenny's arm, which was easier than using her cane, and Jenny remembered to tell her whenever they came to a step. Jenny led her to the stacks and filled her arms with books. They found a table, and Jenny began to search.

Caitlin fidgeted. She heard Jenny turn pages and sigh. She heard her open a different book.

"I could swim in the Paralympics," Caitlin said to break the silence.

"You could," Jenny agreed.

"I might do them anyway," Caitlin said. "They might be fun."

"Sure," said Jenny.

Activity continued

"The only problem is," Caitlin continued, "to swim in the Paralympics, I'd still have to swim straight." Caitlin had decided that she could probably learn to swim straight and slow. Her question was, could she learn to swim straight and fast? As fast as she used to swim? Faster?

Jenny sighed. "I'm not finding anything here. It doesn't look as if any blind swimmers have ever made it to the Olympics."

Caitlin felt so disappointed she nearly cried. "I just don't want to be the first," she said.

"Why not?" Jenny asked. "Why does it matter?"

"It just does." It did matter. If no one else had done it, maybe it couldn't be done.

"Listen to this," Jenny said. "There's something here about a shooter—"

"A *shooter*?"

"Target shooting. With a rapid-fire pistol. Károly Tákacs, from Hungary, won the gold medal in 1948 and 1952. This says that before that, in the 1930s, he was the European pistol champion."

"So?"

"So in between, his right hand got blown off by a grenade. He was right-handed. When he won the Olympics, he shot with his left hand."

Caitlin couldn't even write her name with her left hand. "Wow."

"Yeah." Jenny turned a few more pages. "Here's another one! Equestrian—the first female dressage medalist ever, Lis Hartel from Denmark. She had polio. She couldn't feel her legs from the knees down. She couldn't walk."

"But she could ride," Caitlin said. She felt hope rising like a bubble in her chest.

"You can't see . . . " Jenny said.

Activity continued

"But I can swim." She could learn to swim straight and fast. She could learn where the walls were. It would be hard, but she felt ready, now, to take on the challenge.

"I've missed you at practice," Jenny said. "With you around, I had someone to try to beat."

"Now I'll try to beat you." Caitlin was grinning. "I'll be at practice tomorrow."

They put away the books. Caitlin held her friend's arm. Outside the library, she felt the hot sun. She closed her eyes and imagined, perfectly, water-blue.

1. When Caitlin swims for the first time after the accident, how does she feel?

   _____

   _____

   _____

2. Jenny and Caitlin had never been close friends before the accident. Why do Jenny and Caitlin become good friends now?

   _____

   _____

   _____

Activity continued

3. Why is it important for Caitlin to find out that a blind swimmer had made it to the Olympics?

_____

_____

_____

4. Read the paragraph below.

> They put away the books. Caitlin held her friend's arm. Outside the library, she felt the hot sun. She closed her eyes and imagined, perfectly, water-blue.

At the end of the selection, Caitlin imagines the water-blue. What do you think this means?

_____

_____

_____

_____

5. What is the theme of this story? Use your own words to write the theme.

_____

_____

_____

_____

Apply to the Test

Directions: Use the selection you just read to answer questions 1-5.

1. What does Caitlin hope to achieve in this story?

    A. She hopes to get her sight back.

    B. She hopes that one day she will win the Olympics.

    C. She hopes to be able to swim a straight line fast again.

    D. She hopes to be the second best swimmer on the Junior team.

2. Caitlin sat in the moving car and tried to imagine the color blue. Light blue, shining and deep, like the clear water of a swimming pool. Caitlin tried hard. She knew she should be able to remember what things looked like. She had only been blind for two months, and she had been able to see for twelve years. In her mind she could picture the green of the hills around her home. She could imagine her baby sister's dark brown hair. But light blue, perfect water-blue, always eluded her.

    Why does Caitlin try so hard to visualize what the color blue looks like?

    A. Blue is the color that she wants to remember.

    B. This will help her to not bump into the walls and lane markers when swimming.

    C. Blue is the only color she can't remember and she wants to remember it.

    D. She believes that if she can visualize blue, then she can swim without hitting the walls and lane markers.

3. What does blue represent to Caitlin?

    A. her dreams of success

    B. her ability to succeed

    C. her teammates and friends

    D. the color of the sky

4. At the end of the story, Caitlin can see the color blue because she has

    A   regained her sense of sight.

    B. regained her confidence.

    C. gained a place on the team.

    D. gained a new friend.

5. Jenny and Caitlin became friends because they both wanted something. What did they want from one another and how did they get it? Write your answer on a separate sheet of paper.

LA-D-F-5.6

Fiction is narrative writing. It is a type of literature that is imagined by the author. Fiction has made-up characters and events. It can be based on real life or it can be a fantasy.

Literature contains **dialogue**. Dialogue is the words characters say to one another. In novels, short stories, folktales, and legends, these words are in quotation marks. Some works of fiction have illustrations or pictures to show what is happening in the story.

Here are some types of fiction:

A **novel** is long story whose length is usually between one hundred and five hundred book pages—but it can be longer. Often, a novel has **chapters** and many characters.

A **short story** is a short work of literature. Often, a short story can be read in one hour or less. Usually, it has fewer characters than a novel.

A **play** or **drama** is a story that is performed by actors for an audience. A play can be performed on a stage, on television, or even radio. Plays can also be read for personal enjoyment.

Realistic fiction is a story that seems real, but the characters and events are imaginary. The events in this type of literature could happen to real people.

Historical fiction consists of novels, short stories, or plays set during a real historical era. Historical fiction may contain some actual historical characters or events but the story is made up.

A **folktale** is a story that has no known author. Folktales are passed down from one generation to another by word of mouth. Folktales come from different countries. In general, folktales are not realistic. They may contain animals that talk and act like human beings. They may contain a contest or strange event designed to teach a truth about life.

A **legend** is a story of amazing deeds that is also handed down from earlier times. A legend may be based on a real person or event, but the story has been greatly changed and exaggerated. For example, there are many legends about the exploits of Davy Crockett, a real person, but many of the events have been made up or exaggerated.

Measuring Up® to the Ohio Academic Content Standards

A **myth** is a story that explains something about the world and typically involves gods or other supernatural forces.

Poetry is a kind of rhythmic, concentrated language that uses figures of speech and imagery designed to appeal to your emotions and imagination. Here are some types of poems:

- A **ballad** is a song or songlike poem that tells a story. Often, a ballad is sung.
- A **narrative poem** tells a story in verse.
- A **lyric poem** expresses the feelings or thoughts of a speaker, rather than telling a story.

Nonfiction is literature that tells about real people, events, and places. It provides information about the world. It can also provide directions that tell you how to do things. Here are some types of nonfiction:

- An **essay** is a short piece that examines a single subject.
- A **biography** is an account of a person's life, or part of it, written by someone else.
- An **autobiography** is an account of a person's life written by that person.
- An **informational article** is a piece of writing whose main purpose is to give information.
- An **interview** is a written record of a meeting in which a person is asked about personal views, activities, etc. Often, the interviewer is a newspaper or magazine reporter.

Directions Read the article below. Then answer the questions that follow it.

Wilma Rudolph
by Judith P. Josephson

At the 1960 Summer Olympic Games in Rome, Italy, the United States relay team trailed the German team. Star sprinter Wilma Rudolph grasped the baton from her teammate and shot forward. Her long legs quickly shifted into a scissorslike forward motion. Arms pumping, muscles straining, she edged closer to the German runner. The crowd roared and leapt to their feet as Wilma raced across the finish line—four yards ahead of her opponent.

Wilma Rudolph had just become the first American woman to win three gold medals in one Olympic Game. Personally, she had accomplished something close to a miracle.

A Long, Hard Road

Born June 23, 1940, in rural St. Bethlehem, Tennessee, Wilma was the twentieth child in a family of twenty-two children. She once joked, "I had to be fast. Otherwise, there was nothing left to eat on the table."

Wilma weighed just four and one-half pounds at birth and was sickly. Her parents worried that she might not live. Her health improved for a short time. But then she caught double pneumonia (a serious lung disease), followed by scarlet fever and a mild case of polio. The polio caused her left leg to shrink. Doctors told her that she might never walk again.

Wilma's family surrounded her with love and care. They massaged her crippled leg four times a day. Once a week, Wilma and her mother took the bus to a hospital in Nashville for heat and water therapy.

Wilma's leg slowly improved. When she was eight years old, her leg was fitted with a heavy brace. Wilma was finally able to walk, although her walking was more like hopping. When Wilma was nine, doctors replaced the brace with a high-top shoe. The shoe allowed her to walk more easily. But both the brace and orthopedic shoe reminded her that something was wrong with her.

Activity continued

Despite her difficulties, Wilma did not give up. "'I can't' are two words that have never been in my vocabulary," Wilma said years later. "I believe in me more than anything in this world."

Wilma's corrective shoe did not stop her from playing basketball with her brothers. When the bulky shoe felt too awkward, she took it off and played barefoot.

Wilma grew very tall. When she was sixteen, she was nearly six feet tall and weighed less than one hundred pounds. Her long arms and legs earned her the nickname "Skeeter" (short for mosquito).

But Wilma's height and the skills she had learned playing basketball with her brothers proved to be benefits. Wilma made the all-state basketball team during all four years of high school. She also set a Tennessee state scoring record for girls' basketball. In one game, she scored 49 points!

Wilma also competed in local and state track meets. She qualified for the 1956 Olympic Games in Melbourne, Australia. At the games, she won a bronze medal in the 400-meter relay.

After graduating from high school, Wilma enrolled at Tennessee State University on a track scholarship. Wilma won all of her races for the next three years and became the star of the Tigerbelles track team.

Nobody Came Close

With her classic style and grace, Wilma exploded out of the starting block with raw power and fluid motion. Yet, Wilma's coach talked about her calm temperament. Between races, she even took catnaps. Wilma said once, "Any time I can catch a nap—even for a few minutes—I will."

In many of Wilma's races, the other runners weren't even close to her. In some races, she was so far ahead that she slowed down in the middle of the race to shout encouragement to her teammates.

When she was twenty, Wilma and three of her Tigerbelle teammates went to the 1960 Summer Olympics in Rome. Wilma's performance in Rome smashed records.

Activity continued

In the 100-meter race, she tied the world record of 11.3 seconds. She won a gold medal in that event and also in the 200-meter race, where she set an Olympic record of 23.2 seconds. As the anchor of the 4 × 100-meter relay team, Wilma won her third gold medal and made Olympic history.

Fastest Woman in the World

After the Olympics, everyone was talking about Wilma Rudolph—the fastest woman in the world. When Wilma came home to Clarksville, the town showered her with flowers, a parade, and a banquet.

Wilma continued to compete in track-and-field events until she was twenty-two. Many sports experts believe that if she had continued to compete, she would have accomplished even greater feats. But, at that time, track-and-field performers could not legally accept money for their accomplishments in the sport.

After her retirement, Wilma continued to lead an active life. She worked briefly as a track coach a DePauw University in Greencastle,

Activity continued

Indiana. She acted as the United States's Goodwill Ambassador to French West Africa. She also hosted a radio show, was a spokeswoman for Minute Maid Orange Juice, and served as an executive for a baking company, a bank, and a hospital.

But children were Wilma's special interest. She created the Wilma Rudolph Foundation in Indianapolis, Indiana, to teach underprivileged children how to overcome obstacles and follow their dreams. She considered the foundation to be her greatest achievement.

A Hero to Today's Stars

Wilma Rudolph was the first of many great female American sprinters. She remains the idol of many present-day runners. One of Wilma's admirers referred to her as "an inspiration."

Wilma Rudolph packed much into her fifty-four years before she died of brain cancer in 1994. A legend in her own time, she opened doors for young women to compete in sorts. She also worked for the people she believed in most—children.

As a tribute to her sportsmanship, discipline, and greatness, the Olympic flag draped her casket. There's no doubt, she is truly one of the most well-respected and highly regarded athletes in history.

1. Read the paragraph below.

    > Wilma Rudolph had just become the first American woman to win three gold medals in one Olympic Game. Personally, she had accomplished something close to a miracle.

    What major achievement do you learn about in this paragraph?

    _____

    _____

Activity

2. What type of nonfiction literature is this? How do you know?

   _____

   _____

3. Read the paragraph below.

   > Born June 23, 1940, in rural St. Bethlehem, Tennessee, Wilma was the twentieth child in a family of twenty-two children. She once joked, "I had to be fast. Otherwise, there was nothing left to eat on the table."

   The author includes some of Wilma's exact words to help you understand her. What do you learn about her from her own words in the paragraph above?

   _____

   _____

4. Read this sentence.

   > "'I can't' are two words that have never been in my vocabulary."

   Under which part of the story do you find this sentence?
   What is one event from Wilma's life that supports these words?

   _____

   _____

   _____

Activity continued

5. Based on this selection, do you think that Wilma Randolph is someone to admire? Why or why not?

_____

_____

Apply to the Test

Directions: Use the article you just read to answer questions 1–5.

1. Which statement below BEST explains why this selection is an autobiography?

   A. It contains a fictional character who is a track star.

   B. It tells about the life of a real-life person and was written by someone other than this person.

   C. It tells about someone who was born in St. Bethlehem, Tennessee in 1940.

   D. It was written by someone telling about her own life and experiences.

2. Which of the following does NOT indicate that this selection is nonfiction?

   A. It tells when Wilma Randolph was born and when she died.

   B. It tells how many medals Wilma Randolph won.

   C. It includes Wilma Randolph's exact words.

   D. It shows how people can overcome difficulties.

3. Why does the author include Wilma's statement that she tries to catch a nap between races any time that she can?

    A. to show that she needs more energy

    B. to show that she has a calm temperament

    C. to indicate that she sleeps too much

    D. to prove that she works very hard to reach her goals

4. Which statement below BEST expresses the author's opinion about Wilma Randolph?

    A   "When the bulky shoe felt too awkward, she took it off and played barefoot."

    B. "When she was sixteen, she was nearly six feet tall and weighed less than one hundred pounds."

    C. "There's no doubt, she is truly one of the most well-respected and highly regarded athletes in history."

    D. "Wilma won all of her races for the next three years and became the star of the Tigerbelles track team."

5. Explain why Wilma retired from sports when she was still young. Would you have made the same decision? Why or why not? Write your answer on a separate sheet of paper.

Understand Word Choice and Mood

LA-D-G-5.7

Authors **choose words** carefully. Pay attention to an author's choice of words. Words can help build a mood, show how a character thinks, feels, or speaks, or get across the author's message more clearly. **Concrete nouns** and **vivid verbs** help readers form clear pictures in their minds and create strong impressions. For example:

> The weather forecaster predicted a **blizzard**.
>
> The weather forecaster predicted a **bad storm**.

The first sentence uses a vivid noun. It helps readers create a mental picture.

> "I'll catch you yet!" the villain **hissed**.
>
> "I'll catch you yet!" the villain **said**.

The first sentence uses a vivid verb. It helps readers see how the villain looks and feels.

Authors also choose words and phrases that appeal strongly to the senses. These words are called **sensory words**. These words help readers see, hear, taste, touch, and even smell what is described with words. Some words can appeal to only one sense. Some words appeal to some or all the senses. For example:

> The campers awoke to the **crackling of eggs** in the frying pan and the **whiff of coffee** brewing over the campfire.

Can you almost hear and smell the eggs frying and the coffee brewing?

Words work together to suggest **a mood** or feeling. For example, notice how the words in the sentences below create a mysterious mood.

> The spectral moon lit the old deserted house with the pale eerie light. The weeping willows guarding the path cast black shadows and hung their heads as if in mourning.

Activity

Directions Read the selection below. Then answer the questions that follow it.

The Bogeys of Old Lucky Mine
by Joann Mazzio

Outside the old Lucky Mine, the sun shone brightly. But inside the tunnel of our family's mine, my brother Owen and I saw only dim candlelight.

Each candle flame lighting the tunnel was no bigger than my thumb. It made a little splotch of light against the wall. But the shadows were blacker than pitch.

Owen and I sat with our backs against a wooden timber that held up the roof. We kept our eyes on the candles. Owen whispered, "What if there are bogeys here, like Grandpa says?"

"Naw," I whispered back. "Grandpa is talking about the spirits in the mines in Wales in the old days. It's 1920 now, and we're in America. There aren't any bogeys here."

Owen curled close into my side. Under his breath, he chanted, "Richard, Richard, Richard," as though my name were a charm to keep away bad things. He was only five years old and he was scared.

I was scared, too, even though I'm almost twice Owen's age. Something mysterious was happening to the candles in our mine.

We had begged Dad to let us find out what was happening. He had said we could watch quietly at this end of the tunnel while he and Uncle David worked at the other end. Since we had bragged that we could solve the mystery, we couldn't act scared now and run home. We couldn't even get out the lantern I had hidden behind a big slab of rock. We had to be still as stones and wait.

From around a bend in the tunnel came the echoes of a pick and shovel striking rock. Dad and Uncle David were digging out silver ore at the mine face.

Before the Great War, Dad and my uncle had been coal miners in Wales. They'd worked in a proper old mine with electric lights and a thousand workers and so many tunnels that a body could get lost.

Activity continued

Old Lucky Mine had only one tunnel. And it didn't have electric lights. Dad and Uncle David had driven the pointed ends of iron candleholders into the rock walls. Dozens of white candles lighted the way as they pushed the mine car full of ore through the tunnel to empty it outside.

But for the last two days the candles had been disappearing. From a distance, Uncle David would see a candle flame float up and down along the floor of the tunnel. When he followed it, the flame went out, and he'd be left in darkness until he lit the miner's lamp on his hat.

Owen jerked at my coat sleeve. I saw the same thing he did. A flickering candle flame moved down the side of the wall. It bobbled up and down a few times, then went out.

"Awk," Owen cried and hid his face against my shoulder.

Another candle flame blinked out as though the wind had blown it. I heard a scrabbling sound. Maybe Grandpa was right. Maybe one of those Welsh bogeys was in our family mine.

I tried to talk myself out of being scared. It couldn't be a spirit, I thought. It had to be something real that made the scrabbling sound. Even if Owen and I were scared, we had to try to find out what was really happening.

Owen's warm body scrunched against me. That was real. I heard Dad and Uncle David working. That was real.

There was another noise, closer—a scritchy, sandy sound. It moved to the candle nearest us.

I stretched my eyes wide so I wouldn't blink. In the last instant before the flame went out, I saw a big pack rat snap its yellow teeth shut on the candle.

I jumped up excited and laughing. "Dad," I yelled. "I know what it is!"

Then something clawed onto my leg and wouldn't let go. In the total darkness I couldn't see what it was.

I shook my leg. I tried to lift my foot, but I couldn't. It's a bogey, I thought wildly. Or a snake. A baby dragon. A troll!

Activity continued

I remembered my lantern. I dragged my foot until I reached the slab of rock. Then I groped for the lantern. I raised the little shutter, and the light blazed out to show Owen wrapped around my leg, holding on for dear life.

I pried his hands loose. He put them over his eyes and curled into a ball on the floor.

"Owen, it's not a bogey," I said. "It's just a big old rat."

Dad and Uncle David ran up with their lanterns and the miner's lamps glowing on their hats. Light washed over us.

"Rat? Did you say rat?" Dad asked.

"Yep," I said, "we solved the mystery. Rats are stealing the candles."

Dad threw back his head and laughed and then punched Uncle David on the arm as though they were kids. Uncle David laughed, too.

Dad said, "Why didn't we think of that, David?"

"It's been a cold winter, and they must have run out of food," said Uncle David. "They're taking the candles to eat."

"We can trap them," I said.

"No," Dad said, "we don't want to kill them. As long as rats can live in our mine, we know the air is safe to breathe."

Owen said, "Richard and I will stay here every day and guard the candles. I'm not afraid of any big old rat."

"I have a better idea," said Uncle David. "We'll make wire guards to go around the candles."

"Won't the rats starve?" I asked.

"If you and Owen bring them bread every day, they'll stay in the mine."

"I'm going to the house right now to tell Grandpa there aren't any bogeys," Owen said. He ran toward the entrance as fast as he could.

"I'll come with you and get some bread and candles," I called after him. Now that the mystery was solved, I, too, wanted to get outside and wash away the darkness with the sunshine.

Activity continued

1. Read the paragraph below.

> Each candle flame lighting the tunnel was no bigger than my thumb. It made a little splotch of light against the wall. But the shadows were blacker than pitch.

To which of the five senses do the details in the paragraph above mostly appeal?

_____

_____

2. Read the paragraph below.

> Owen curled close into my side. Under his breath, he chanted, "Richard, Richard, Richard," as though my name were a charm to keep away bad things. He was only five years old and he was scared.

Which detail in the paragraph above appeals mostly to the sense of hearing? How does this detail increase the suspense?

_____

_____

3. Read the paragraph below.

> "I'll come with you and get some bread and candles," I called after him. Now that the mystery was solved, I, too, wanted to get outside and wash away the darkness with the sunshine.

How does the mood of the story change at the end? Which detail tells you this?

_____

_____

Activity continued

4. Read the paragraph below.

> Old Lucky Mine had only one tunnel. And it didn't have electric lights. Dad and Uncle David had driven the pointed ends of iron candleholders into the rock walls. Dozens of white candles lighted the way as they pushed the mine car full of ore through the tunnel to empty it outside.

Which details in the paragraph above appeal to the sense of sight? Which appeal to the sense of hearing?

_____

_____

_____

_____

5. To make a story lively, you need to include vivid words that describe what things are like or how they happen. On the lines below, make a list of the liveliest words you can think of. Then, use some in a story that you make up and tell. Write your story on a separate piece of paper.

_____

_____

_____

_____

_____

_____

Apply to the Test

Directions: Use the selection you just read to answer questions 1–5.

1. Since we had bragged that we could solve the mystery, we couldn't act scared now and run home. We couldn't even get out the lantern I had hidden behind a big slab of rock. We had to be still as stones and wait.

   In the paragraph above, the author builds suspense by including details that appeal mostly to the sense of

   A. sight

   B. smell

   C. taste

   D. hearing

2. Owen jerked at my coat sleeve.

   In the sentence above, the author uses the vivid verb **jerked** to suggest that Owen is

   A. calm

   B. cold

   C. nervous

   D. mean

3. Owen's warm body **scrunched** against me.

   In the sentence above, the word **scrunched** means

   A. knocked

   B. sat

   C. fell

   D. crouched

4. Which sentence below from the story creates a ghostly atmosphere?

    A   "They'd worked in a proper old mine with electric lights and a thousand workers and so many tunnels that a body could get lost."

    B. "From a distance, Uncle David would see a candle flame float up and down along the floor of the tunnel."

    C. "Dad and Uncle David were digging out silver ore at the mine face."

    D. "Dad threw back his head and laughed and then punched Uncle David on the arm as though they were kids."

5. At first, why does it seem that there might be bogeys in the mine? What is the real cause behind the bogeys? Write your answer on a separate sheet of paper.

Understand Figurative Language

LA-D-G-5.8

Do words always mean exactly what they say? Not always! **Figurative language** is language that is not meant to be taken literally, or at face value. Writers use figurative language to make their writing effective and visual. Figurative language stirs the imagination and helps you see things in new and surprising ways. Two types of figurative language are **similes** and **metaphors**.

A **simile** is a comparison between two different things using words such as like or as. Similes help readers picture the things being described. For example:

> An angry look flashed across his face like lightning in a dark sky.
>
> The skin of the whale is as slippery as wet soap.

A **metaphor** also compares two different things, but without using like or as. For example:

> When the peacock spreads its wings, it is a rainbow of color.
>
> The still lake is the sun's hand mirror.
>
> The snow on the street is a fluffy blanket.

Personification means giving human qualities to nonhuman things. For example:

> The gentle moon whispered, "good night."
>
> The vast ocean called the sailors to sea.

An **idiom** is an expression whose meaning is different from what you may find in a dictionary. You cannot find the meaning of an idiom by looking up each word in a dictionary. These expressions are often found in common everyday language. The expressions themselves have a specific meaning that is common to a particular culture or language. For example:

> Go back to the drawing board.
>
> It is written all over your face.

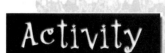

Directions Read the selection below. Then answer the questions that follow it.

Riding the Whale
by Liz Gallagher

My parents make me ride around in the most embarrassing car. I call it the Blue Whale. It's a station wagon, light blue and huge. There's a fake-wood stripe along each side, like scars from some sea battle.

Dad thinks that the car is dependable.

Mom told me that everyone used to have station wagons. I imagine long ago, when the Blue Whale and other huge cars traveled through herds of dinosaurs.

I'm sitting in the back seat, and it smells like our attic.

I shouldn't say that the Blue Whale smells like our attic. It's not our attic anymore. We're not even going to have an attic where we're going.

My parents are moving me from the suburbs, from my house, from my school, from my friends.

We are moving into the city, and the Blue Whale is taking us there.

"Mom," I say. "Let's get a sport utility vehicle, like everybody else."

Mom tells me that she loves the Blue Whale. "Do you remember the trip we took when we bought this car? It was your first time at the beach."

I sigh. "Mom, how far is the beach from the city?"

She doesn't answer. I'm hoping she just didn't hear me.

We stop in a traffic jam. This road is always full of cars. Every time my parents take me to the art museum or to a baseball game, we get trapped in traffic. I'm usually so annoyed.

Now, we're trapped on our way to the new apartment. I don't mind.

I close my eyes. Cars going the other way are still moving. They rush past our car. Through my open window, their sound is like the ocean. Each car's passing is a new wave.

Activity continued

That sounds like something my teacher would have said. She was always telling us to think about the world.

Here's something else she told me: "You are a turtle. Wherever you go, you have all you need, like a turtle with everything in its shell."

Of course, we learned in science class that a turtle doesn't really have anything in its shell except its body. But at first, I pictured a cartoon turtle, with his bed, his toothbrush, and his sport utility vehicle inside his shell.

And then I realized what my teacher was saying. She was saying that all I ever need to be happy is my body, my brain, myself.

I'm glad I have my parents, too.

The traffic begins moving again. "Thank goodness," Mom says.

"Looks like we'll make it there before dark," Dad says.

I'm hoping that all this traffic was caused by one of our moving trucks stalling or being abducted by space aliens—or anything else that might put off this move.

I wish that I were floating in the ocean, being carried by waves. But instead, I'm inside the Whale.

Once, I floated for so long that I didn't realize that the tides were taking me down the shore. I thought I was stationary, like a buoy, bobbing up and down in my own spot in the water. I thought I was staying in front of my family's spot on the beach, the one we always picked, next to Jimmy's Hot Dog Haven.

I expected to swim in to shore looking at Jimmy's red-and-white striped umbrella. I thought that my biggest challenge would be avoiding jellyfish.

But when I turned myself upright, I had no clue where I was. I didn't see my parents. Or Jimmy's hot-dog stand. Or any jellyfish, which was the only good thing.

I saw an unexpected sight—Charlie's Chicken Stand. I felt like screaming.

Activity continued

I started swimming to shore anyway. It was only a minute before I saw my parents waving at me. They were out of breath, and I later found out it was from running down the beach, looking for me. I'd floated pretty far down the shore.

That day, we tried Charlie's Chicken Stand. I didn't get my Super Jimmy Dog, but it was one of the best meals of my life because I had found my new favorite—the Charlie Clucker.

Now, I look out the window, and I see another unexpected sight. The city's skyline is shining. The sun is about to set, and the horizon is orange and pink. It looks as if a giant seashell has taken the whole big city inside itself . . . like a pearl, maybe.

I wonder where we'll eat dinner tonight. I wonder when this new spot will feel like home.

Suddenly, I'm excited to figure this place out. But it won't be like floating anymore or like being carried in the Blue Whale. I am going to swim through the city. I am going to explore.

"We're almost there," I say. "What should we do first?"

1. Read the paragraph below.

> Mom told me everyone used to have station wagons. I imagine Long Ago, when the Blue Whale and other huge cars traveled through herds of dinosaurs.

Sometimes people use figurative language to name things. How is the car like a whale? What impression do these words in the paragraph above create of the station wagon?

_____

_____

_____

Activity continued

2. Read the paragraph below.

> My parents are moving me from the suburbs, from my house, from my school, from my friends.

Which words in this paragraph help you understand how the narrator feels about the fact that he or she is moving away from everything he or she cares about?

_____

_____

_____

3. Read the paragraph below.

> I close my eyes. Cars going the other way are still moving. They rush past our car. Through my open window, their sound is like the ocean. Each car's passing is a new wave.

The author uses figurative language to emphasize how far the narrator is moving from the ocean. What simile does she use to describe the sound of the cars going in the opposite direction? What metaphor does she use? Explain the simile and metaphor.

_____

_____

_____

_____

Activity continued

4. Read the paragraph below.

> It looks as if a giant seashell has taken the whole big city inside itself . . . like a pearl, maybe.

Explain the figurative language in this sentence.

_____

_____

5. Look at the story structure. Complete each sentence below to show how the narrator feels about moving to a new place in the beginning, the middle, and the end of the story.

First the narrator feels

_____

_____

Then the narrator remembers how he/she had the best meal of his or her life when he/she

_____

_____

Finally the narrator feels

_____

_____

Apply to the Test

Directions: Use the selection you just read to answer questions 1–5.

1. There's a fake-wood stripe along each side, like scars from some
    sea battle.

    What impression of the car does this simile create?

    A. It has been near the water.

    B. It is worn from hard use.

    C. It is very expensive.

    D. It is well cared for.

2. Here's something else she told me: "You are a turtle. Wherever you
    go, you have all you need, like a turtle with everything in its shell."

    What is the teacher suggesting by comparing the girl to a turtle?

    A. She should stay close to home.

    B. She should never take risks.

    C. She has everything she needs.

    D. She should learn to swim.

3. Once, I floated for so long that I didn't realize that the tides were taking me down the shore. I thought I was stationary, like a buoy, bobbing up and down in my own spot in the water. I thought I was staying in front of my family's spot on the beach, the one we always picked, next to Jimmy's Hot Dog Haven.

What impression does the detail of the buoy create?

A. security

B. danger

C. peacefulness

D. annoyance

4. Now, I look out the window, and I see another unexpected sight. The city's skyline is shining. The sun is about to set, and the horizon is orange and pink. It looks as if a giant seashell has taken the whole big city inside itself . . . like a pearl, maybe.

What impression do the details in this paragraph create of the city?

A. It seems like a frightening place.

B. It seems like an exciting place.

C. It seems like an unattractive place.

D. It seems like a noisy place.

5. How does the narrartor feel when she turns right-side-up and sees Charlie's Chicken Stand? What does he/she do and why? Write your answer on a separate sheet of paper.

     Measuring Up® to the Ohio Academic Content Standar

LA-D-A-5.1, LA-D-B-5.2, LA-D-C-5.3, LA-D-D-5.4,
LA-D-E-5.5, LA-D-F-5.6, LA-D-G-5.7, LA-D-G-5.8

Directions: Read the selection.

Señor Coyote and the Tricked Trickster
A tale from Mexico retold by Linda K. Garrity

One day long ago in Mexico's land of sand and giant cactus *Señor* Coyote and *Señor* Mouse had a quarrel.

None now alive can remember why, but recalling what spirited *caballeros* these two were, I suspect that it was some small thing that meant little.

Be that as it may, these two took their quarrels seriously and for a long time would not speak to each other.

Then one day Mouse found Señor Coyote caught in a trap. He howled and twisted and fought, but he could not get out. He had just about given up when he saw Señor Mouse grinning at him.

"Mouse! *Mi Viejo amigo*—my old friend!" he cried. "Please gnaw this leather strap in two and get me out of this trap."

"But we are no longer friends," Mouse said. "We have quarreled, remember?"

"Nonsense!" Señor Coyote cried. "Why I love you better than I do Rattlesnake, Owl, or anybody in the desert. You must gnaw me loose. And please hurry for if the *peon* catches me I will wind up a fur rug on his wife's kitchen floor."

Mouse remembered how mean Señor Coyote had been to him. He was always playing tricks on Mouse and his friends. They were funny to Señor Coyote for he was a great trickster, but they often hurt little Mouse.

"I'd like to gnaw you free," he said, "but I am old and my teeth tire easily."

"Really, Señor Mouse, you are ungrateful," said Señor Coyote reproachfully. "Remember all the things I have done for you."

"What were they?"

"Why—" Coyote began and stopped. He was unable to think of a single thing. There was good reason for this. He had done nothing for Mouse but trick him.

But Señor Coyote is a sly fellow. He said quickly, "Oh, why remind you of them. You remember them all."

"I fear my memory of yesterday is too dim," Mouse said, "but I could remember very well what you could do for me tomorrow."

"Tomorrow?" Coyote asked.

"Yes, tomorrow. If I gnaw away the leather rope holding you in the trap, what will you do for me tomorrow, and the day after tomorrow and the day after tomorrow and the day—"

"Stop!" Señor Coyote cried. "How long is this going on?"

"A life is worth a life. If I save your life, you should work for me for a lifetime. That is the only fair thing to do."

"But everyone would laugh at a big, brave, smart fellow like me working as a slave for a mere mouse!" Señor Coyote cried.

"Is that worse than feeling sad for you because your hide is a rug in the peon's kitchen?"

Señor Coyote groaned and cried and argued, but finally agreed when he saw that mouse would not help him otherwise.

"Very well," he said tearfully, "I agree to work for you until either of us die or until I have a chance to get even by saving your life."

Mouse said with a sly grin, "That is very fine, but I remember what a great trickster you are. So you must also promise that as soon as I free you that you will not jump on me, threaten to kill me, and then save my life by letting me go!"

"Why, how can you suggest such a thing!" Coyote cried indignantly. And then to himself he added, "This mouse is getting *too* smart!"

"Very well, promise," Mouse retorted.

"But I am not made for work," Señor Coyote said tearfully. "I live by being sly."

"Then be sly and get out of the trap yourself," Mouse retorted.

"Very well," Señor Coyote said sadly. "I will work for you until I can pay back the debt of my life."

And so Mouse gnawed the leather strap in two and Coyote was saved. Then for many days thereafter Señor Coyote worked for Mouse. Mouse was very proud to have the famous Señor Coyote for a servant. Señor Coyote was greatly embarrassed since he did not like being a servant and disliked working even more.

There was nothing he could do since he had given his promise. He worked all day and dreamed all night of how he could trick his way out of his troubles. He could think of nothing.

Then one day Baby Mouse came running to him. "My father has been caught by Señor Snake!" he cried. "Please come and save him."

"Hooray!" cried Coyote. "If I save him, I will be released from my promise to work for him."

He went out to the desert rocks and found Señor Rattlesnake with his coils around Señor Mouse.

"Please let him go and I will catch you two more mice," Coyote said.

"My wise old mother used to tell me that a bird in hand is worth two in the bush," Snake replied. "By the same reasoning, one mouse in Snake's stomach is worth two in Coyote's mind."

"Well, I tried, Mouse," Coyote said. "I'm sorry you must be eaten."

"But you must save me, then you will be free from your promise to me," Mouse said.

"If you're eaten, I'll be free anyway," Coyote said.

"Then everyone will say that Coyote was not smart enough to trick Snake," Mouse said quickly. "And I think they will be right. It makes me very sad for I always thought Señor Coyote the greatest trickster in the world."

This made Coyote's face turn red. He was very proud that everyone thought him so clever. Now he just *had* to save Mouse.

So he said to Snake, "How did you catch Mouse anyway?"

"A rock rolled on top of him and he was trapped," Mouse said. "He asked me to help him roll it off. When I did he jumped on me before I could run away."

"That is not true," Snake said. "How could a little mouse have strength to roll away a big rock. There is the rock. Now you tell me if you think Mouse could roll it."

It was a very big rock and Coyote admitted that Mouse could not possibly have budged it.

"But it is like the story *Mamacita* tells her children at bedtime," Mouse said quickly. "Once there was a poor burro who had a load of hay just as large as he could carry. His master added just one more straw and the poor burro fell in the dirt. Snake did not have quite enough strength to push the rock off himself. I came along and was like that last straw on the burro's back and together we rolled the rock away."

"Maybe that is true," Snake said, "but by Mouse's own words, he did only very little of the work. So I owe him only a very little thanks. That is not enough to keep me from eating him."

"Hmmm," said Coyote. "Now you understand, Snake, that I do not care what happens myself. If Mouse is eaten, I will be free of my bargain anyway. I am only thinking of your own welfare for both of us. I don't need your thoughts."

"Thank you," said Señor Rattlesnake. "but I do enough thinking about my welfare for both of us. I don't need your thoughts."

"Nevertheless," Coyote insisted, "everyone is going to say that you ate Mouse after he was kind enough to help you."

"I don't care," Snake said, "Nobody says anything good of me anyway."

"Well," said Coyote, "I'll tell you what we should do. We should put everything back as it was. Then I will see for myself if Mouse was as much help as he said he was or as little as you claim. Then I can tell everyone that you were right, Snake."

"Very well," said Señor Snake. "I was lying like this and the rock was on me—"

"Like this?" Coyote said, quickly rolling the rock across Snake's body.

"Ouch!" said Snake. "That is right."

"Can you get out?" Coyote asked.

"No," said Snake.

"Then turn Mouse loose and let him push," said Coyote.

This Snake did, but before Mouse could push, Coyote said, "But on second thought if Mouse pushes, you would then grab him again and we'd be back arguing. Since you are both as you were before the argument starts, let us leave it at that and all be friends again!"

Then Coyote turned to Mouse. "So, my friend, I have now saved your life. We are now even and my debt to you is paid."

"But mine is such a *little* life," Mouse protested. "And your is so much *larger*. I don't think they balance. You should still pay me part."

"This is ridiculous!" Coyote cried. "I—"

"Wait!" Snake put in hopefully. "Let me settle the quarrel. Now you roll the rock away. I'll take Mouse in my coils just the way we were when Coyote came up. We'll be then in a position to decide if—"

"Thank you," said Mouse. "It isn't necessary to trouble everyone again. Señor Coyote, we are even."

Directions: Use the selection to answer questions 1–10.

1. Which statement below BEST explains why this story is a folktale?

   A. This story is meant to be performed for an audience by actors.

   B. This story is passed down from one generation to another.

   C. This story tells about events that actually happened.

   D. This story involves gods and goddesses and other supernatural forces.

2. "Nonsense!" Señor Coyote cried. "Why I love you better than I do Rattlesnake, Owl, or anybody in the desert. You must gnaw me loose. And please hurry for if the peon catches me I will wind up a fur rug on his wife's kitchen floor."

   When you read this paragraph, you know that Señor Coyote

   A. is very fond of Mouse.

   B. does not mean what he is saying.

   C. dislikes Rattlesnake and Owl.

   D. wants to leave the desert.

3. "My wise mother used to tell me that a bird in hand is worth two in the brush," Snake replied.

   Which saying below means almost the same thing as the saying above?

   A The early bird catches the worm.

   B. Be satisfied with what you have, not what you hope for.

   C. Don't cry over spilt milk.

   D. Without risk, there is no gain.

4. "But mine is such a *little* life," Mouse protested. "And your is so much *larger*. I don't think they balance. You should still pay me part."

Which of the following BEST describes Mouse?

A. greedy

B. forgiving

C. foolish

D. generous

5. Give two reasons why Mouse does not want to help Señor Coyote at first. Write your answer on a separate sheet of paper.

6. Where in Mexico does this folktale take place?

A. in a desert

B. on a riverbank

C. in the mountains

D. in someone's backyard

7. Señor Coyote groaned and cried and argued, but finally agreed when he saw that mouse would not help him otherwise.

The author uses vivid verbs in the sentence above to show that Señor Coyote

A. was in great physical pain.

B. did not want to help Mouse.

C. regretted all his past misdeeds.

D. was eager to assist a friend.

8. How did Señor Coyote come to be Señor Mouse's servant?

    A. Señor Snake tricked Señor Coyote into being a servant for Señor Mouse.

    B. Señor Coyote promised to be a servant to Señor Mouse for freeing him from a trap.

    C. Señor Mouse wanted nothing more than to be a servant to Señor Coyote.

    D. They paid each other back for favors done by being servants to one another.

9. This made Coyote's **face turn red.**

    The idiom in the sentence above suggests that Coyote is

    A. embarrassed.

    B. sad.

    C. tired.

    D. happy.

10. On a separate sheet of paper, compare and contrast how Señor Coyote and Señor Mouse are alike and how they are different. Remember to include at least two details from the story to support your answer.

Chapter 4 Informational, Technical, and Persuasive Texts

What's Coming Up?

In this chapter, you will learn how to:

- use text features;
- analyze information in graphics;
- read instructions;
- understand cause and effect;
- identify facts and opinions;
- find main ideas and summarize;
- understand author's purpose;
- analyze arguments and persuasive techniques;
- draw conclusions.

Nonfiction

Nonfiction provides information about the read world. It tells you facts and provides data about real people, real events, and real things. Autobiographies, biographies, magazines, newspapers, and reference books are forms of nonfiction reading. When you read nonfiction, you can find out about a topic that interests you or you can learn how to solve problems. You can understand how to do something or how something works.

Nonfiction Is All Around You!

Nonfiction may tell you about the first flight to the moon or about the origin of our number system. It may tell you about a current events topic or the life of your favorite novelist. When you read nonfiction, read at a comfortable rate. Read slowly and carefully when you are reading about a new topic, or if you find the book difficult to read.

There is so much nonfiction available to readers that the modern age has been dubbed "the information age." You can find nonfiction articles in newspapers, magazines, and on the Web. Television and radio broadcast nonfiction. Books, flyers, and brochures contain nonfiction articles, as well. Reading, listening, or viewing nonfiction is important to learn more about the world.

Chapter 4 Informational, Technical, and Persuasive Texts

Activity

Directions Read each situation. Then identify the type of source you would use to find the information. You can list more than one source.

Situation	Source
How to play chess	_____
	_____
What is the Loch Ness monster?	_____
	_____
Where is Peru? Facts about Peru	_____
	_____
Who is Sammy Sosa?	_____
	_____
Where is he from?	_____
	_____
What has he achieved?	_____
	_____
How to do a multimedia presentation on a computer	_____
	_____

Measuring Up® to the Ohio Academic Content Standards

Strategies for Reading

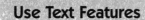

LA-C-A-5.1, LA-C-A-5.5, LA-C-A-5.6, LA-C-B-5.2, LA-C-B-5.7,
LA-C-C-5.4, LA-C-D-5.9, LA-C-E-5.8, LA-C-E-5.9, LA-C-F-5.3

When you read nonfiction, apply reading strategies to improve your understanding and fluency. Use these strategies to comprehend a broad range of reading materials.

Use Text Features

Nonfiction books have special **features**, or **organizers**, to help you better understand the information presented in the text. These include a table of contents, an index, and graphic aids. Nonfiction text features can help you sort and keep track of information.

Analyze Information in Graphics

Graphic aids, such as tables, graphs, charts, maps, and diagrams add or explain information in the main text.

Nonfiction also has very specific **text structures**. A text structure is an organizational pattern an author uses to present information. Knowing how to identify text structure will help you to better understand and remember what you read. Different kinds of text structures include the following:

Read Instructions

Some nonfiction texts contain **instructions** about how to do something. When you read instructions, follow the proper sequence of the steps.

Understand Cause and Effect

A cause is the reason why something happens. An **effect** is the result, or what happens. When you read, look for cause-and-effect relationships.

 Identify Facts and Opinions

A **fact** is information that can be proved. An **opinion** is information that cannot be proved because it expresses a personal feeling or judgment. For example, it is a fact that Earth is a planet in the solar system. It is an opinion that Earth is by far the most interesting of all the heavenly bodies in the universe.

 Find Main Ideas and Summarize

The topic is the subject, or what a piece of writing is about. The **main idea** is the most important idea about the topic. **Supporting details** back up, or support, the main idea. When you **summarize**, find the most important information and restate it in your own words. Summarize every time you study to help you understand and remember what you read. Compare and contrast the main ideas of articles about the same topic.

 Understand Author's Purpose

An author has a **purpose** or reason for writing. It may be to inform, to explain, to persuade, or even to entertain. The author chooses information and arranges it in a certain way based on this purpose.

 Analyze Arguments and Persuasive Techniques

An **argument** provides reasons for taking a certain position or recommending a certain action. **Persuasive techniques** are the methods the author uses to get you to agree with him or her.

 Draw Conclusions

When you draw **conclusions**, you add up the information from what you read to reach a decision. This decision is based on evidence from the article. To draw a conclusion, look at the treatment, scope, and organization of ideas.

READING GUIDE

Directions Put your strategies to use as you read. The questions in the margin will guide you.

Sandra on Sports
by Sandra Neil

1 *What if I pass out right now? I think. What if I forget what I'm supposed to say?*

"Thirty seconds to air . . ." the producer's assistant counts down.

"Have a good show, everybody," barks the producer.

"We are live in twenty . . ."

Breathe, Sandra, I say to myself. Deep breaths, in and out. Live television is just like life, you breathe in and out, and it just happens.

"Ten seconds . . ."

"I know it's cold in this rink, Sandra, but don't forget to smile," the producer reminds me. His voice is way too loud in my ear-piece, but my hands are trembling, and I can't find the volume knob to turn it down.

"Five . . . four . . . three . . . two . . . We're on!"

2 "Hello, I'm Sandra Neil. Welcome to the Skate International Champions Series on Fox Sports."

3 I'm clutching the microphone with both hands. Words somehow come out of my blue lips, painted red by the makeup artist. I can feel the blood slowly returning to my cheeks. I am in the midst of my first sports broadcast.

My Early Years

Long before that day in the ice rink, I began my career during college, reporting on news stories at a Toronto radio station. The station's program manager

GUIDED QUESTIONS

1 **Text Features** What text feature helps you identify the writer's thoughts?

2 **Main Idea** What is this article about?

3 **Author's Purpose** What is the author's purpose for writing this article?

READING GUIDE

GUIDED QUESTIONS

was also a professor who taught one of my classes. I convinced him that he needed a youth reporter because that year was International Youth Year. After graduation, I took a job as a television news reporter and later, news anchor. But sports reporting was something different, so I decided to try it. Figure skating was my first assignment.

4 **Getting Ready**

I had two months until I began my new job. It was like waiting an entire summer for school to start. There was plenty of time to be reminded that instead of three hundred thousand viewers, I would be seen by millions of people across the United States.

5 I spent those two months talking to figure-skating coaches and judges. I read boring rule books. I drove to the rinks where the skaters trained, and made notes about our conversations. I even took a lesson, which made some of the skaters laugh. So on the night of my first broadcast, once the nerves left me, I relied on my new knowledge and told the stories I had learned.

Help from an All-Star

6 My second assignment was the National Hockey League All-Star game in Boston. I was to be the first woman on television to cover NHL hockey.

"What gives you the right to cover hockey?" said a stale voice behind my back during the morning practice session.

I turned around to face the veteran sports writer who had spoken those angry words, but I was too stunned to respond.

A player shot the puck in my direction. *Whack!* It hit the glass beside me, rattling the boards. I didn't flinch, but I'd had enough for one morning. Being a

4 **Text Features** How does this heading help you identify what the two paragraphs under it will be about?

5 **Summarize** Summarize the information in this paragraph.

6 **Fact and Opinion** Does this paragraph contain facts or opinions? How do you know?

woman rookie sportscaster was tougher than I'd imagined. I didn't know that my childhood idol, Hall of Famer Bobby Orr, would be on my side.

7 Some say Bobby Orr was the greatest defenseman to ever play hockey. He completely changed the meaning of his position. For a hundred years defensemen didn't score. They stayed behind the blue line, goalies' best friends. But Bobby saw things differently. He could get the puck, skate past opponents all the way to the other net, then score! He played for thirteen years before retiring because of a knee injury.

I was standing near the locker rooms before the game when I bumped into Bobby.

"First time covering a hockey game?" he asked, smiling.

"Yeah."

"Piece of cake. You'll be great."

Bobby Orr said I'd be great! That thought gave me a burst of confidence.

"And if anyone gives you a hard time, tell them to talk to me!" he added.

And with that, Bobby Orr walked out on the ice and dropped the ceremonial puck to start the All-Star evening. The fans let out a huge roar. Inside, I roared, too. Then I heard my producer through my headset.

"Get an interview ready for the next whistle."

A Tough Job

8 Being a reporter during a sports broadcast is tougher than hosting one. You do just as much preparation, but you only speak when someone gets injured or the game becomes boring. Then you have to get all the information out in twenty seconds.

7 **Fact and Opinion** Which sentence in this paragraph expresses an opinion?

8 **Argument** Does the author convince you that being a reporter during a sports broadcast is tougher than hosting a broadcast? Explain.

READING GUIDE

GUIDED QUESTIONS

9   **Here I am holding the Stanley Cup at the Hockey Hall of Fame. If you think it looks heavy, you're right. It weighs thirty-five pounds.**

9 Graphics Based on the photograph and the caption, how do you think Sandra feels?

Later on, while reporting on my first NBA game, I was so pumped that I jumped over the bench and joined the huddle, listening to the home team's instructions. The coach stopped talking. The players all started laughing. Then the coach told me to stay behind the bench, like the rest of the reporters, unless I could play point guard. I turned as red as a tomato.

10   But I don't usually get nervous anymore. After four years, I'm a familiar face around rinks and courts. And you know, I've never heard from that sarcastic sports writer again. Most of the people I meet now are as friendly as Bobby Orr.

10 Author's Purpose Do you think the author did a good job of showing what it is like to be an on-line sports reporter? Explain.

LA-C-A-5.1

Nonfiction books contain special features that help you find information. Here are some examples:

The **table of contents** appears in the front of a book. It lists the book's chapters, in order, and usually **chapter titles**. The table of contents also gives the page number where each chapter begins. By reading the chapter titles, you can see what kind of information the book contains.

The **index** and **glossary** are at the back of a nonfiction book. The index is an alphabetical list of all names and subjects in the book. Page numbers follow each entry, letting the reader know where information can be found. A glossary is like a mini-dictionary. It contains words in alphabetical order that are important to the book. (Not all nonfiction books have glossaries.).

Now let's look inside a nonfiction book. Many nonfiction books or textbooks contain text organizers. Here are some examples:

The **titles, headings**, and **subheadings** of a nonfiction book are like main ideas. They tell what the section, or part, of the text is about. Sections may be divided into subsections, or smaller sections. Subheadings provide a title for each smaller chunk of information. Headings and subheadings remind you of what you just read and may be useful when looking for answers to questions.

The size of the heading matters. Large type headings are more important than smaller type headings. Boldface or color headings are more important than lightface headings. Some headings get a special type treatment to make that stand out.

Informational text may include **illustrations** or **photographs**. These features provide additional visual information.

Captions give information about a visual. **Labels** and **callouts** point out specific details in the text or illustrations. **Sidebars** give more information about a topic mentioned in the main text.

Nonfiction books often have **graphic aids**, such as diagrams, graphs, or charts that add or explain information in the text.

You may see words or headings in *italics* or in **boldface**. Some words may even be in **color**. These are important words that the author wants you to remember or learn.

Finally, if you still need more information, you can use **search engines** to locate addition information about a topic on the Internet. Type in a **keyword** to find different sites that might be helpful. The keyword may name a topic or subtopic.

Directions Read the table of contents below. Then answer the questions that follow it.

Table of Contents
Ancient Mexico

1. If you wanted to find information about a particular city, in which part of the book would you look?

_____

2. In what chapter would you find information about Palenque?

_____

3. How many chapters does the book include about different peoples who lived in ancient Mexico?

_____

Activity

Directions Read the selection below. Then answer the questions that follow it.

The Man Who Painted Truth
by Kathleen M. Hayes

Oscar Howe was a Native American artist who was born on South Dakota's Crow Creek Reservation in 1915. Could his paintings be both modern and true to his heritage?

Oscar Howe sat quietly at his drawing table, concentrating on a piece of blank paper. He was looking for what his Dakota Sioux ancestors called "points of beauty." After a while, he picked up his pencil and began to connect the imaginary points with delicate lines. Gradually the picture in his mind appeared in the maze of lines on the paper.

Although points of beauty were an important part of an ancient Dakota ceremony, Howe's paintings looked modern. Too modern, many people thought. All of his life he struggled to convince others that his paintings could be both modern and true to his heritage.

Lines of Magic and Beauty

Oscar Howe was born on South Dakota's Crow Creek Reservation in 1915. Starting at age three, he began to draw lines on paper. "Each line had a fascination for me," he said. "I though of magic and beauty."

Oscar's parents did not understand his lines. The lines were abstract and did not seem to represent familiar objects like people and animals.

Activity continued

His parents took away his pencil and paper, so Howe began to draw with charcoal. When they forbade him to draw with charcoal, he drew on the ground outside. Though he was very young, Howe had already begun to develop his own artistic vision and style.

Studio Style

Howe attended high school in New Mexico, where he won a place in the Santa Fe Indian School's painting program. The program became world famous as the Studio. It was run by Dorothy Dunn. Dunn encouraged Howe and the other students to paint subjects from their tribal backgrounds. She taught everyone to draw with firm outlines and little or no shading. She taught them to keep background details to a minimum and to use natural colors. The style Dunn taught became the style all Native American painters were expected to use.

Finding His Own Truth

Early in his career, Howe painted in the Studio style. He painted pictures of Sioux boys on horseback, buffalo hunts, and deer bounding across the prairie. But as he became more confidant, his work began to change.

He experimented with the traditional "point-and-line" technique of Dakota painters. Designs were created from point to point. Curved or straight lined connected each point. The pictures that emerged were filled with geometric shapes and bursting with color and emotion. They were not at all like the pictures he had learned to paint at the Studio.

Critics complained that his new style looked too modern to be Native American. Howe disagreed. "I have taken the straight line out of the Dakota past and used it as a part of my art," he said. "Its meaning remains the same—the truth." In Dakota pictographs and sign language, a straight line stood for truth. Howe had begun to paint his own truth.

Activity continued

Howe returned to the reservation often to talk to the old people. "I heard the truth from them and responded by painting them in like manner of their words," he said. But his work continued to draw criticism. In 1958, he submitted a painting to a Native American art competition. The painting was rejected. The judges did not think it fit the rules for Native American art.

Howe wrote a letter of protest to the museum: "Are we to be held back forever . . . with no right for individualism, dictated to as the Indian has always been . . . ?"

His words made museum directors, art critics, and teachers all over the world stop and think. Shouldn't Native American artists be treated like other artists, free to paint as they wished?

Changing Native American Art

The next year, the museum changed its rules to allow different styles of painting for their competition. Howe was awarded the grand prize. In his independent way, he had won a battle as dramatic as any fought by his Dakota ancestors.

"In art I have realized a part of a dream," Howe once said. "To present a true image of the Dakota Indian as I understood him and his culture." By the time of his death in 1983, Oscar Howe's efforts to paint his vision of the truth had forever changed Native American art.

The Painting of the Truth

Oscar Howe's way of painting draws on a traditional Dakota ceremony. It is called "the painting of the truth." During the ceremony, an artist, a relater, and witnesses work together to document an important event.

For three days before the ceremony, the artist studies the painting area to choose points of beauty. During the ceremony, the relater describes the event. The artist draws and paints what the relater has described.

In traditional Dakota art, pictures begin with points of beauty. The artist creates a design by connecting these points with straight or curved lines. Straight lines represent truth. Curved lines symbolize unity, movement, and the open sky.

Howe used this method in his art to express the lifeway of his people.

Activity

1. Look at the headnote, the boxed text that begins this article. Rewrite the question in your own words.

   _____

   _____

2. Read the paragraph below. Underline the concluding sentence. Rewrite it in your own words.

   > Although points of beauty were an important part of an ancient Dakota ceremony, Howe's paintings looked modern. Too modern, many people thought. All of his life he struggled to convince others that his paintings could be both modern and true to his heritage.

   _____

   _____

   _____

3. Look at the section with the heading **Studio Style**. In what way was what Dorothy Dunn expected like what Oscar's parents expected?

   _____

   _____

4. Which heading do you think means "finding what is important or meaningful to him"?

   _____

   _____

     Measuring Up® to the Ohio Academic Content Standard

Activity continued

5. Nonfiction that tells about real people sometimes contains their exact words. Read the following words that Howe wrote in a letter: "Are we to be held back forever . . . with no right for individualism, dictated to as the Indian has always been . . . ?"

Rewrite Howe's words in your own words

_____

_____

Apply to the Test

Directions: Use the selection you just read to answer questions 1–5.

1. According to the sidebar, which of the following explains how Howe used a straight line in a way that connected him to his heritage?

   A. He used it to represent truth.

   B. He used it to symbolize powerful emotions.

   C. He used it to show movement.

   D. He used it to describe the open sky.

2. In the sections called "Finding His Own Truth" and "Changing Native American Art," what was the effect of Howe's letter of protest?

   A. He was given the award.

   B. He was barred from the contest.

   C. The museum changed its rules the next year.

   D. The museum stopped holding the contest.

3. Which heading from the article tells you that the section will be about how Howe was taught to paint in school?

   A. Lines of Magic and Beauty

   B. Studio Style

   C. Finding His Own Truth

   D. Changing Native American Art

4. The information under the heading "Lines of Magic and Beauty" is mostly about

   A. the meaning of "points of beauty."

   B. Howe's last years.

   C. critics reaction to Howe's new style.

   D. how Howe painted when he was a child.

5. After reading this article and looking at the illustration, do you think that Howe's paintings were both modern and true to his heritage? Use at least two details from the article to support your response. Write your response on a separate sheet of paper.

LA-C-A-5.5

Most textbooks and other works of nonfiction contain **graphic aids**, such as **charts**, **tables**, **graphs**, **diagrams**, and **maps**.

A **chart** is a useful tool for organizing information and data. A chart has a title that tells what it is about. It also has columns and rows that are usually labeled. Charts allow you to compare two or more things. **Tables** and **schedules** are kinds of charts.

A **table** is an arrangement of numbers or facts. Most tables are arranged with vertical and horizontal rows and columns. A table groups numbers or facts and puts them into categories.

A **diagram** is a special type of drawing that illustrates a place, how to do something, or steps of a process. A diagram can also show the parts of something. When you study a diagram, pay attention to the arrows, labels, and callouts.

A **graph** is a visual display of ideas and statistics. It presents data in a highly organized, easy-to-understand manner. Three types of graphs are circle or pie charts, bar graphs, and line graphs.

A **map** is a drawing or a diagram of a place. A map may show the entire world, a country, a state, or a city. There are different types of maps for different purposes. To make information on maps understandable, maps contain special features. These features may include one or more of the following:

- a title
- symbols (pictures, shapes, or colors that stand for the real things)
- a map key
- a compass rose
- a scale
- captions or labels
- inserts

Activity

United Nations
A Community of Nations
from *The World Almanac for Kids 2004*

The United Nations (UN) was started in 1945 after World War II. The first members of the UN were 50 nations that met in San Francisco, California. They signed an agreement known as the UN Charter. By early 2003, the UN had 191 independent countries as members—including East Timor, which joined in 2002. Only two independent nations—Taiwan and Vatican City—were not members.

The UN Charter lists these purposes:

- to keep worldwide peace and security
- to develop friendly relations among countries
- to help countries cooperate in solving problems
- to promote respect for human rights and basic freedoms
- to be a center that helps countries achieve their goals

Fast Facts About the UN

UN Day is celebrated every year on October 24, the day the UN Charter was ratified by a majority of nations.

- The flags of all 191 members—from Afghanistan to Zimbabwe—fly in front of UN Headquarters in New York and UN European Headquarters in Geneva, Switzerland.
- Six official languages are used at the United Nations—Arabic, Chinese, English, French, Russian, and Spanish.
- The UN is the world's only organization permitted to issue postage stamps. Usually only countries are allowed to do that. UN stamps can be used only to send mail from UN offices in New York, Geneva, and Vienna.
- The land and buildings of the UN Headquarters in New York City are officially international territory. The 18 acres of land were donated by John D. Rockefeller, Jr. in 1945.

Activity continued

> • The UN's office in Vienna, Austria, is the home of the United Nations Office for Outer Space Affairs (UNOOSA), which is responsible for promoting international cooperation in the peaceful uses of outer space.

Did You Know?

Before there was a UN, there was the League of Nations, a similar organization founded in 1919, after World War I, in an effort "to promote international cooperation and to achieve peace and security." The U.S. never joined. After failing to prevent World War II, the League of Nations disbanded, transferring all of its assets to the UN in 1946. Beneath the foundation stone of the Palais des Nations, the UN's European Headquarters in Geneva, Switzerland, is a box containing a list of League of Nations members as of 1929 and coins from each country.

UN Peacekeepers

The Security Council sets up and directs UN peacekeeping missions, to try to stop people from fighting while the countries or groups try to work out their differences. The map shows the location

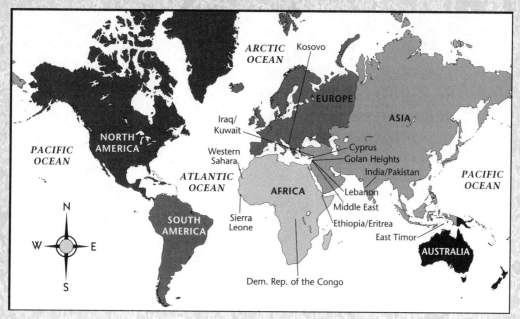

Activity continued

of 13 peacekeeping missions that were operating in January 2003. These peacekeepers wear blue helmets or berets with white UN letters. In 2001, the UN approved a special mission for Afghanistan, the International Security Assistance Force (SAF). In early 2003, more than 4,000 troops were based in Kabul, with support from 22 countries. These troops work under UN authority, but don't wear UN berets.

How the UN is Organized

Organization of UN	What It Does	Members
General Assembly	discusses world problems, admits new members, appoints the secretary-general, decides the UN budget	All members of the UN belong to the General Assembly; each country has one vote.
Security Council	handles questions of peace and security	Five permanent members (China, France, Great Britain, Russia, U.S.), each of whom can veto any proposed action; ten elected by the General Assembly for two-year terms. In early 2003 the ten were Bulgaria, Cameroon, Guinea, Mexico, and Syria (ending 2003) and Angola, Chile, Germany, Pakistan, and Spain (ending 2004).

Measuring Up® to the Ohio Academic Content Standar

Activity continued

Economic and Social Council	deals with issues related to trade, economic development, industry, population, children, food, education, health, and human rights	Fifty-four member countries elected for three-year terms.
International Court of Justice (World Court) located at The Hague, Netherlands	highest court for disputes between countries	Fifteen judges, each from a different country, elected to nine-year terms.
Secretariat	carries out day-to-day operations of the UN	UN staff, headed by the secretary-general.

For more information about the UN, you can write to: Public Inquiries Unit, United Nations, Room GA-57, New York, NY 10017. Web site: www.un.org.

Activity continued

1. Find the chart that provides fast facts about the UN. How many flags fly in front of the UN? How many acres of land were donated by John D. Rockefeller, Jr.?

   _____

   _____

2. Find the box with the heading "Did You Know?" What similar organization came before the UN? What is in the box beneath the foundation stone of the Palais des Nations?

   _____

   _____

3. Find the map showing UN Peacekeepers. Is East Timor closer to Australia or to Sierra Leone?

   _____

4. If you wanted to find information about what the security council does, what feature in this article would you look at?

   _____

5. Suppose you were doing a report on the UN. You want to find the most up-to-date information about peacekeeping missions. What two sources mentioned in this article could you use?

   _____

   _____

Apply to the Test

Directions: Use the article you just read to answer questions 1–5.

1. Which organ of the UN is mainly responsible for the day-to-day operations of the UN?

    A. the Security Council

    B. the Economic and Social Council

    C. the World Court

    D. the Secretariat

2. If you traveled from Ohio in the United States to Europe, in which direction would you go?

    A. north

    B. south

    C. east

    D. west

3. If you wanted to find out to which nations the UN did NOT send peacekeepers in 2003, under which heading would you look?

    A. Fast Facts About the UN

    B. Did You Know?

    C. UN Peacekeepers

    D. Organization of UN

4. The Democratic Republic of the Congo is located on which continent?

   A. North America

   B. South America

   C. Africa

   D. Asia

5. Why do you think the United States is called "A Community of Nations"? Use at least two details from the article and your own ideas to support your answer. Write your response on a separate sheet of paper.

LA-C-A-5.6

Instructional texts provide **directions** on how to do something. They may tell you how to set up or use equipment, how to make something, or how to repair something. Recipes, how-to guides, and technical manuals are different types of instructional text.

Authors also use text features, or organizational patterns, to present information. Text features include **sequence**. Often, instructional text is organized in **sequential order**. You follow the steps in correct order. Always start at number one.

Study **illustrations** or **diagrams**. These are special types of pictures that visually help to explain the steps. You may need to also read labels carefully. Remember, **labels** point out specific details in the text or illustrations.

When you read instructions, make sure they are complete. They should tell you how to do something from beginning to end.

 **Directions** Read the instructions below. Then answer the questions that follow it.

10 STEPS TO START FISHING

1. KEEP IT SIMPLE. All you need is a fishing pole and reel, a small spool of fishing line (6 to 8 pound test), a couple of plastic bobbers, some split shot sinkers (BB size), and some hooks (size 2 up to size 3/0). A tackle box with a handle will help keep it all organized.

2. BAIT. You can buy night crawlers, minnows, or crickets at a bait shop. But it is more fun to catch your own. Carry your bait in a small plastic bucket.

3. Prepare your pole and reel for the day of fishing. Make sure all parts are in working order.

4. Match a hook to the bait. Use a 3/0 hook for large worms and a 1/0 for minnows. Tie the hook to the end of your line using a knot that won't slip.

Activity continued

5. Now you are ready to go fishing. A pond is your best bet if you live inland. Most are loaded with bluegills and bass. Piers and large rocks close to shore are better if you live on the coast.

6. After baiting your hook, attach the bobber above the hook (two feet for starters). Lower the hook into the water until the bobber floats. Hold your pole steady.

7. Wait for the fish to bite. FISHING TAKES PATIENCE! Watch the bobber—if it jumps or shakes, a fish is nibbling your bait.

8. When your bobber goes completely under water, set the hook. This is done by raising the pole quickly. Reel in the fish with care.

9. Once the fish is landed, handle it with care. Most fish caught from shore don't have sharp teeth, but may have spiny fins. Hold the fish firmly and remove the hook. A needle-nose pliers may be needed.

10. This is a good time to get a picture of your catch. Then release the fish back into the water gently. The fish will swim away, grow bigger, and be there for another day of fishing.

Better Fishing

- An inexpensive and rugged reel to start with is the spincast outfit. You can pick up a good one (around $10) at any tackle or discount store, or have your parents purchase one online.

- Practice your casting skills. Use an open area with no trees or power lines. Practice plugs are best suited for practicing. Place a target on the ground about 25 feet in front of you. Extend your arm with the rod pointed at the target, bend your arm back until the rod is at the 1 o'clock position, then snap your arm forward while releasing the button at the same time.

- Use the best lures. Most fish will bite a lure that looks like a minnow, crayfish (crawdad), or other living prey. Spinnerbaits, crankbaits, and plastic worms work best for bass. Trout, pike, and saltwater fish will hit shiny metal lures. Use a tackle box or a utility box to hold your lures. Remember that the hooks are sharp.

       Measuring Up® to the Ohio Academic Content Standard

Activity continued

- Normally fish hide around cover. Cover can be anything from weeds and trees to logs and rocks. Don't be afraid to cast into this good stuff. Most strikes will occur on the drop when the lure passes by the cover or bumps into the cover. You may lose a few lures when fishing cover, but you'll catch more fish.

- Vary the retrieve speed to make the lure look more realistic.

- When a fish strikes, you need to set the hook. The second you feel a tap on the line, lower the rod tip, reel up the slack, and sharply jerk the rod upward.

- When fishing heavy cover, where the bigger fish normally live, use a plastic worm or a "jig and pig" (leadhead jig with a pork frog trailer). Cast into the thickest area of the cover, let the lure drop, then shake the rod tip gently to coax a bite.

- Topwater lures are the most exciting to fish. These lures float on the surface. When fishing with a topwater, cast near the cover, let it set for several seconds, then twitch the rod tip so the lure works on the surface. When done correctly you will experience a KA-SPLOOSH—the surface explodes as the fish bites your lure.

- When fishing is tough or slow, try using a smaller lure. A 4-inch worm is a good choice. Rig the worm on a 1/0 hook with a BB-size split-shot weight attached to the line about 18 inches above the hook. Cast the lure out and wait for it to settle on the bottom. Work, or reel, it very slow. The weight will bounce on the bottom, causing the worm to dart in different directions.

- After you master the spincast outfit, try a more precise spinning or baitcaster. Spinning reels are ideal for clear water using 4 to 10 pound test line. The baitcaster is best for big, strong fish. Use line with a 12 to 30 pound test.

- Fishing is more fun when you share it with a friend or parent. Show a beginner how you learned to cast, tie knots, and select lures.

Activity continued

1. Explain why it is important to follow the instructions in the order they are presented before actually fishing.

    _____

    _____

2. How many steps does it take to complete a specialist fly knot? What features does the author provide to make this process easy to follow?

    _____

    _____

3. In addition to explaining what a **spincast outfit** and a **lure** do, what does the author do to help you visualize these instruments?

    _____

    _____

4. Under the heading "10 Steps to Start Fishing," why are the words "KEEP IT SIMPLE," "BAIT," and "FISHING TAKES PATIENCE!" written in capital letters? What do these words mean?

    _____

    _____

    _____

5. Were these instructions intended for a beginner or expert fisher? Explain.

    _____

    _____

Apply to the Test   **Directions: Use the instructions you just read to answer questions 1-5.**

1. Which type of lure is BEST to attract bass fish?

    A. trout

    B. minnow

    C. spinnerbaits

    D. living prey

2. Another good heading for the section "Better Fishing" would be

    A. Choosing the Best Lure to Catch Big Fish.

    B. Tips For Improving Your Fishing Technique.

    C. Professional Fishing Challenges.

    D. Learn How to Cast, Tie Knots, and Select Lures.

3. All of the following will hit shiny metal lures EXCEPT

    A. freshwater fish.

    B. trout.

    C. pike.

    D. saltwater fish.

4. The steps in the section "10 Steps to Start Fishing"

   A. should be followed in the order in which they appear.

   B. should be completed before you begin fishing.

   C. are not important for learning how to fish.

   D. are only for experienced fishermen.

5. Explain whether these instructions are helpful. Be sure to include at least two details from the instructions in you response. Write your response in a separate sheet of paper.

Copying is illegal. Measuring Up® to the Ohio Academic Content Standard

Understand Cause and Effect

LA-C-B-5.2

Authors also organize information to show cause-and-effect situations. A **cause** is the event or action that makes something happen. An **effect** is what happens, or results, because of an event or action. When you read informational text, make sure you can tell the difference between a cause and an effect.

How can you recognize the cause and the effect? Look for what makes something happen and why it happens. To find the effect, ask **what** happened. To find the cause, ask **why** it happened.

| cause | → | brings about | → | effect |
| door slams | → | brings about | → | jar falling |

An effect may have more than one cause.

cause 1				
cause 2	→	bring about	→	effect
cause 3				
typing skills				
filing skills	→	bring about	→	getting an office job
writing skills				

A cause may have more than one effect.

				effect 1
cause	→	results in	→	effect 2
				effect 3
Tim oversleeps				Tim runs to school.
one morning.	→	results in	→	Tim drops his books.
				Tim is late for class.

Look for **signal words** or **phrases** that show cause and effect. Here are some examples.

as a result	because	so	since	consequently
therefore	due to	for	so that	for this (that) reason
thus	nevertheless	lead/led to	if . . . then	this (that) is how

The disease spread <u>because</u> of poor sanitation.

Effect   *The disease spread*

Cause   *poor sanitation*

Sometimes a cause-and-effect relationship has no signal words. In this case, use the logical sequence of events to determine the cause and effect.

Evan kicked the ball. It rolled down the street.

Effect   Evan kicked the ball.

Cause   It rolled down the street.

By recognizing a cause and effect text structure in a selection, you can better understand and remember things about the information in the text.

Activity

Directions Read the selection below. Then answer the questions that follow it.

Stop That Airliner!
by Peter C. Price

Have you ever watched an airliner landing? The engines are quiet as the pilot glides toward the airport. They roar back to life the moment the wheels touch the runway! You'd think the pilot has decided to take off again. Yet the louder the engines get, the more the plane slows down. The pilot has used thrust reversers.

I started designing passenger planes when jet engines first came into use. These new airliners were sleeker and their engines more powerful. They not only flew faster than propeller planes—they landed faster too! That was a big problem. We had to figure a way to slow the airliner down quickly once it was on the ground. Other planes would be waiting to land or take off. Our plane had to get clear of the runway. Then it had to taxi to the terminal to let its passengers off.

Bigger brakes weren't the answer. They'd need to be enormous! They might get so hot the tires would catch fire! Besides, we couldn't risk the airliner's skidding if it used only brakes on a wet or icy surface. Imagine a spinout on a slippery runway! It would be dangerous. Airliners are bigger, heavier, and faster than cars.

We fitted "slats" and "flats" to make the wings wider and more curved for landing. (Just like the people who'd invented airplanes, we copied birds. Notice how birds slow down to land. They make their

Activity continued

wings wider by extending feathers backwards. They curve them, too.) Slats and flaps weren't enough to slow down these new planes; they were still going to land at 130 miles an hour or more!

I was one of the designers who scratched his head! Then we remembered: It was the thrust of the jet engines that made planes fly fast. Why not turn the thrust around at the end of the flight? Blow it forward instead of backward?

We didn't even try to make the engines run backward; they wouldn't work that way! Besides, you can't stop a spinning, bike wheel and send it whizzing the other way in two seconds. The compressor part of a jet engine is spinning much faster—10,000 times a minute!

Instead, we added doors to the shiny casing that wraps around the engine. (It's called the nacelle.) The pilot pops these doors open the moment he lands, then revs the engines again. The doors block the thrust that's pushing the airliner forward. At the same time, we allow the thrust to escape. Now it's aimed toward the front of the plane; the thrust is reversed!

The turned-around thrust is slowing the plane down. Later, when the airliner is stopped at the terminal, and all the passengers have boarded, pilots use thrust reverse again. They use them to back away from the loading area!

The next time you hear the engines roar as an airliner lands, you'll know why. The pilot has opened the throttles—to slow you down!

Activity continued

1. Why did jet engine planes create more of a problem at airports than propeller planes?

    _____

    _____

2. Why wouldn't bigger brakes solve the problem of slowing the jet plane down? Give three reasons.

    _____

    _____

3. Why did the people trying to solve the problem use "slats" and "flats"?

    _____

    _____

4. Why didn't they try to solve the problem by making the engines run backward?

    _____

    _____

5. Explain how the thrust is reversed.

    _____

    _____

Apply to the Test

Directions: Use the selection you just read to answer questions 1–5.

1. Thrust reversers cause the airplane to

   A. take off.

   B. speed up.

   C. slow down.

   D. make less noise.

2. Jet planes had to clear the runway fast because

   A. other planes were waiting to get off.

   B. they were sleeker than propeller planes.

   C. the terminals were very far away.

   D. travelers preferred jet planes to propeller planes.

3. Why does the pilot pop the door around the engine open when he or she lands on the runway?

   A. to let the passengers out

   B. to block the thrust

   C. to let the thrust out

   D. to make the plane move faster

4. Why does the pilot use thrust reversers after the passengers have boarded the plane?

    A. to stop the plane

    B. to start the engines

    C. to make the plane move faster

    D. to back away from the terminal

5. Explain why the people trying to solve the problem of stopping jet planes observed birds. Use details from the article to support your response. Write your response on a separate sheet of paper.

LA-C-B-5.7

You know that an author can use an organizational pattern to present information. Another kind of text structure is fact and opinion. A **fact** is an objective statement that can be proved true. For example:

> Neil Armstrong was the first human to walk on the moon.
>
> He traveled to the moon in 1969 aboard Apollo 11.

These statements are facts. You can check the information in encyclopedias, history books, and almanacs to prove them true.

An **opinion** is a subjective statement that cannot be proved. It is a person's judgment or belief about something. For example:

> Neil Armstrong was the bravest astronaut who ever lived.
>
> Traveling to the moon is the scariest thing a person could do.

These statements are opinions. They cannot be proved. Some people might think that Neil Armstrong is the bravest astronaut who ever lived. Others might not. Some people might believe that traveling to the moon is the scariest thing a person could do. Others might not. These statements express the writer's personal feelings about Neil Armstrong's journey to the moon.

Sometimes there are words that signal opinions, such as *think, believe, feel, strongly, probably, the best*, and *the most*.

Identifying facts and opinions helps you to **read critically**. For example, read the advertisement at left.

This ad uses both facts and opinions. When the ad says that the pie is the best in Ohio, it is giving an opinion. It tells what someone thinks and believes and cannot be proven correct. When the advertisement states the ingredients, these are the facts. You can prove whether this information is correct.

Activity

Directions Read the article below. Then answer the questions that follow it.

Reaching for the Sky
by Kim Williams

Have you ever looked at a building and thought, "I wish I could design a building like that"? That's how I used to feel.

In the 1950s, when I was young, I lived in Houston, Texas. As I grew up, the city grew up. To me, the most exciting changes were those you could see on the skyline. One big building after another went up. When visitors came, we always took them downtown to show them the latest skyscraper.

I think that's what made me want to be an architect. To me, those buildings actually did scrape the sky, and I wanted to have a part in building one. I used to spend hours building cities with my Lego blocks. I loved being the architect! At first I didn't know what it took to be an architect except that you had to be able to draw. In high school, instead of taking home economics like my friends, I took a class called drafting. There I learned how to use many different tools to draw exact plans for building things.

I was the only girl in the class, and others teased me. But I knew what I wanted to do, so I didn't mind the jokes.

Trans-Alaska Pipeline

When I was sixteen, I found my first summer job with an engineering company. I worked in the drafting room with sixty men on one of the biggest engineering projects of our century: the Trans-Alaska Pipeline. That pipeline now carries oil south across Alaska, from oil wells near the Arctic Ocean down to the Pacific.

That summer I learned a lot about how a huge structure is designed and what it's like to work in a team. The architect leads the team and decides what kind of structure will work best for the job. The architect also chooses the overall artistic idea for the project. Engineers, draftsmen, and many others make up the rest of the team.

Activity continued

As a draftsman, I learned how to turn the architects' and engineers' ideas into drawings. Construction workers then used my drawings to build those parts of the pipeline.

Sometimes, I learned the hard way. If a drawing wasn't right, it had to be done over. Years later, one of my bosses from that summer said he knew that I had what it takes to succeed. He said he could tell because if he told me to start over, I just smiled and sat down to work again.

The engineers liked my work so much that they asked me to come back. I worked there for the next five summers.

During those years, I studied architecture at the University of Texas. I discovered that the best way to learn about architecture is to look at the world around me. To remember what I saw, I kept a notebook handy so I could make quick sketches.

Not all of my classes were easy. There weren't very many women studying architecture at that time. And we were required to do some things that seemed to come easier to the men. For example, we had to learn how to build models, and many of the men had already spent a lot of time building model ships and airplanes when they were young.

The Way Up

After I graduated from college, I set out to make my dream come true. I moved to New York City, where I became one of many young people who hoped to find jobs as apprentice architects.

My summers in the engineering office really paid off. Thanks to my drawing skills, I soon landed my first job. It wasn't very glamorous, not at all as I had imagined it would be. As the youngest person on the staff, I had to do all the things no one else wanted to do—like design the bathrooms!

But one by one I was given more exciting jobs. After I had worked as an apprentice for five years, I took the test to earn my license as a registered architect.

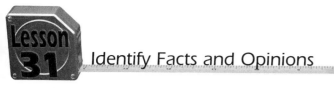

Activity continued

Once I had my license, I was hired to work for a famous architect, Philip Johnson. And I learned how small the world is: one of the skyscrapers I worked on was built in Houston. Now when I go home to visit my family, I see the building that I worked on, and I feel that my dream has come true.

Becoming an Architect

Here are some things you can do to see if you would like to be an architect.

Draw a Room

Draw a plan of your room. Don't forget to show where the doors and windows are! Next, draw in each piece of furniture. Experiment by drawing different arrangements of your furniture. When you color it in, you will have completed your first architectural drawing.

Sketch Buildings

Do a quick sketch from memory of the outside of your school or house. Then compare your drawing with the real thing. Now sketch the building as you look at it. See how much more you notice about it now?

Compare Details

Collect picture postcards of your favorite structures. You'll begin to notice the differences among buildings that were built for different purposes. (How is a theater different from a bank?) And you'll begin to see differences among structures built in various climates. (Why do houses in the Northeast need sloped roofs?)

Even if you don't want to be an architect, I hope you'll try these suggestions. They'll help you see the world as architects do.

Activity continued

1. In your own words, tell Kim Williams's opinion of being an architect.

_____

_____

2. Read the paragraph below.

> In the 1950s, when I was young, I lived in Houston, Texas. As I grew up, the city grew up. To me, the most exciting changes were those you could see on the skyline. One big building after another went up. When visitors came, we always took them downtown to show them the latest skyscraper.

In this paragraph, which sentence states an opinion? Which words are clues that helped you identify this as an opinion?

_____

_____

3. Read the paragraph below.

> Sometimes, I learned the hard way. If a drawing wasn't right, it had to be done over. Years later, one of my bosses from that summer said he knew that I had what it takes to succeed. He said he could tell because if he told me to start over, I just smiled and sat down to work again.

What opinion did Kim's boss have of her? How did he back up his opinion?

_____

_____

Activity (continued)

4. Read the paragraph below.

> I think that's what made me want to be an architect. To me, those buildings actually did scrape the sky, and I wanted to have a part in building one. I used to spend hours building cities with my Lego blocks. I loved being the architect! At first I didn't know what it took to be an architect except that you had to be able to draw. In high school, instead of taking home economics like my friends, I took a class called drafting. There I learned how to use many different tools to draw exact plans for building things.

In this paragraph, you learn an important fact about studying to become an architect. What course did Kim take in school to prepare for the job? How is this different from an art course?

_____

_____

5. Read the sentence below.

> I discovered that the best way to learn about architecture is to look at the world around me.

Circle the word in the sentence above that tells you this is an opinion. Write a statement that expresses a different opinion about learning architecture.

_____

_____

Apply to the Test

Directions: Use the selection you just read to answer questions 1–5.

1. Which of these statements from the selection is an opinion?

   A. "The architect leads the team and decides what kind of structure will work best for the job."

   B. "To me, those buildings actually did scrape the sky, and I wanted to have a part in building one."

   C. "That summer I learned a lot about how a huge structure is designed and what it's like to work in a team."

   D. "At first I didn't know what it took to be an architect except that you had to be able to draw."

2. Which of the following statements is a fact?

   A. I feel that my dream has come true.

   B. I worked on the best team comprised of engineers and draftsman.

   C. But one by one I was given more exciting jobs.

   D. After I had worked as an apprentice for five years, I took the test to earn my license as a registered architect.

3. Which detail below supports Williams's opinion that the architects she worked with during the summer liked her work?

   A. They asked her to come back.

   B. They asked her to do jobs over.

   C. She studied architecture at the University of Texas.

   D. She learned how to turn the architects' ideas into drawings.

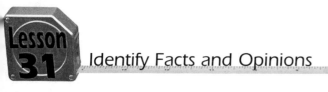

4. Which detail BEST supports the author's opinion that architects do some things that seem to come easier to men?

    A. When she started out, there were not many women in the field.

    B. Williams first job wasn't very glamorous.

    C. Williams worked as an apprentice for five years.

    D. Many of the men in her class had already spent a lot of time building model ships and airplanes when they were young.

5. Did Williams convince you that being an architect is an exciting job? Use at least two details from the article and your own ideas to support your response. Write your response on a separate sheet of paper.

Find Main Ideas and Summarize

LA-C-C-5.4

The **main idea** of a selection is what the selection is about. As you read, ask yourself, "What subject, or topic, is being discussed or described?" and "What is the selection mainly about?" The topic can be anything the author wishes to write about, such as hurricanes, basketball, pollution, computer games, and so on.

The **main idea** is the most important point that an author makes about the topic. The main idea is usually stated in the first paragraph.

Every paragraph in an article can have a main idea, too. Often, the main idea is stated in one sentence, called the topic sentence. Although the topic sentence is often the first sentence, it can be in the middle or end of a paragraph, as well.

The rest of the sentences in the paragraph usually give details about the main idea. These details support or help explain the main idea.

Good readers look for the main idea and details to help them understand and remember the author's most important points and to help them concisely summarize a selection.

Sometimes, the main idea is not stated directly in a paragraph. It is **implied**. A reader must put together details to figure out, or infer, the unstated main idea. For example:

> At the museum, you can see some of the earliest airplanes, including the Wright Brothers plane. There are fighter planes from World War I and World War II. There are examples of American, British, Canadian, German, and Japanese planes. In addition, there are commercial planes from the early days of commercial flight up to the present. There is also a space shuttle and a simulator that helps you feel what it is like to be weightless.

When you put together the details in this paragraph, you can figure out that the main idea is that the museum provides visitors with a vivid picture of the history of flight.

A **summary** is a short statement of the most important ideas in a selection or paragraph. When you **summarize**, you determine the main idea or topic of a selection by looking for a topic sentence or by creating your own based on what you have read. Then you find the most important details in the text or paragraph. Write the summary in your own words. Begin with a topic sentence and include supporting details in order of importance. Do NOT include your own opinions.

Activity

Directions Read the article below. Then answer the questions that follow it.

Why Do Birds Sing?
by Mary Sue Waser

"Keep out or I'll chase you out! This is my property!"

You hear this every spring. We all hear it, and most of us do not pay any attention. Most of us don't understand it because it's not in our language. It is a long musical sound—a birdsong! Birds use their songs to communicate different messages to one another. They also use calls, shorter sounds like "cheep" and "chirp." Calls have different meanings from songs. People who study bird sounds are learning their meanings.

Usually it is the male that sings. Early in spring he sings to say that he has picked out a piece of property. He sings to attract a female of his same kind. Together they will raise a family in his territory. He sings to tell all other birds of his kind to keep out.

Each kind of bird has its own type of song. Cardinals sing something that sounds a little like "What cheer, cheer, cheer." Towhees sing, "Drink your tea." Ovenbirds sing, "Teacher, teacher, teacher." People have thought of

The cardinal's song sounds to us like: "What cheer, cheer, cheer."

these words to help them remember the songs. Most birds sing songs that are too complicated or too fast for words. But with practice you can learn to recognize many birds just by their songs.

Most of the time birds pay attention only to the songs of birds of their own kind. Cardinals answer cardinals, and song sparrows answer song sparrows. When I hear a bird singing from its territory, I often hear another of the same kind singing back. A cardinal knows

Activity continued

that a song sparrow will not try to steal its mate. So you can see one reason why a cardinal may chase away another cardinal but will not bother a song sparrow.

Most different kinds of birds eat different things or hunt for their food in different places. For example, with its heavier bill the cardinal can catch large insects for its young. The smaller song sparrow can take tinier bits of food from smaller places. But two cardinals would look for the same kinds of food in the same kinds of places. So you can see another reason why a cardinal would chase another cardinal from its territory. It probably would ignore a song sparrow since the song sparrow would often be eating other kinds of food.

When I watch my bird feeder, I often see different kinds of birds chasing each other. The feeder offers in one small place a large amount of food that many birds like and can get at easily. By scattering the seeds around on the ground, I can reduce the competition and the chasing.

In the wild, birds fight and chase much less about food. A few seeds are in one place, a few in another. One insect is here, another there.

To find enough to eat for itself and its family, a bird needs a big piece of land to search in. Many kinds of birds have some way of dividing up the land into territories. Song sparrows, cardinals, ovenbirds, mockingbirds, house wrens, white-throated sparrows, and indigo buntings are some of the birds that have territorial systems.

Especially in early spring, birds work out the boundaries between their territories by singing "keep out" threats and by chasing and fighting each other. The birds continue singing to tell females that they have set up territories. Neighboring birds seem to agree that there are make-believe fences between their pieces of property. Then they do not have to waste energy chasing each other instead of taking care of their young.

   Measuring Up® to the Ohio Academic Content Standards

Activity continued

Scientists guessed that some birds could recognize their neighbors by small differences in their songs. In a similar way you might recognize your neighbors if you heard them talk but couldn't see them.

Two scientists who studied white-throated sparrows found that these birds can even tell the difference between songs of individual birds of their own kind. White-throated sparrows have songs that seem to say "I'm your neighbor" or "I'm a stranger" or "I'm your neighbor to the west." Other kinds of birds could tell neighbors from strangers by their songs, too.

The next time you hear a bird singing, listen to it. If it's in early spring, you might hear a bird singing to attract a mate. Perhaps you'll see birds chasing and hear them singing, agreeing on a property line. Later in the spring you may hear two birds answering each other. They are telling their neighbors, their mates, and anyone else who is listening that they are still there.

1. Read the paragraph below.

> Usually it is the male that sings. Early in spring he sings to say that he has picked out a piece of property. He sings to attract a female of his same kind. Together they will raise a family in his territory. He sings to tell all other birds of his kind to keep out.

Which sentence states the main idea in this paragraph?

_____

_____

Activity continued

2. Read the paragraph below.

> You hear this every spring. We all hear it, and most of us do not pay any attention. Most of us don't understand it because it's not in our language. It is a long musical sound—a birdsong! Birds use their songs to communicate different messages to one another. They also use calls, shorter sounds like "cheep" and "chirp." Calls have different meanings from songs. People who study bird sounds are learning their meanings.

What is the most important idea that you learn about birds in this paragraph?

_____

_____

3. Read the paragraph below.

> Most different kinds of birds eat different things or hunt for their food in different places. For example, with its heavier bill the cardinal can catch large insects for its young. The smaller song sparrow can take tinier bits of food from smaller places. But two cardinals would look for the same kinds of food in the same kinds of places. So you can see another reason why a cardinal would chase another cardinal from its territory. It probably would ignore a song sparrow since the song sparrow would often be eating other kinds of food.

Why would a cardinal chase away another cardinal when hunting for food, but not a sparrow?

_____

_____

Activity continued

4. Read the paragraph below.

> Most of the time birds pay attention only to the songs of birds of their own kind. Cardinals answer cardinals, and song sparrows answer song sparrows. When I hear a bird singing from its territory, I often hear another of the same kind singing back. A cardinal knows that a song sparrow will not try to steal its mate. So you can see one reason why a cardinal may chase away another cardinal but will not bother a song sparrow.

What details support the idea that birds pay attention to only the songs of birds of the same sort?

_____

_____

5. Read the paragraphs below.

> Scientists guessed that some birds could recognize their neighbors by small differences in their songs. In a similar way you might recognize your neighbors if you heard them talk but couldn't see them.
>
> Two scientists who studied white-throated sparrows found that these birds can even tell the difference between songs of individual birds of their own kind. White-throated sparrows have songs that seem to say "I'm your neighbor" or "I'm a stranger" or "I'm your neighbor to the west." Other kinds of birds could tell neighbors from strangers by their songs, too.

How can birds tell the difference between songs of individual birds of their own kind?

_____

_____

Lesson 32 Find Main Ideas and Summarize

Apply to the Test

Directions: Use the article you just read to answer questions 1–5.

1. Especially in early spring, birds work out the boundaries between their territories by singing "keep out" threats and by chasing and fighting each other. The birds continue singing to tell females that they have set up territories. Neighboring birds seem to agree that there are make-believe fences between their pieces of property. Then they do not have to waste energy chasing each other instead of taking care of their young.

   Which sentence states the main idea of this paragraph?

   A. "Especially in early spring, birds work out the boundaries between their territories by singing 'keep out' threats and by chasing and fighting each other."

   B. "The birds continue singing to tell females that they have set up territories."

   C. "Neighboring birds seem to agree that there are make-believe fences between their pieces of property."

   D. "Then they do not have to waste energy chasing each other instead of taking care of their young."

2. Which detail does not belong in a summary of this article?

   A. Birds sing in order to attract a mate or establish a property line.

   B. Each type of bird has its own type of song.

   C. Most of us don't pay attention to bird songs.

   D. A bird's song may alert others of its presence.

3. Each kind of bird has its own type of song. Cardinals sing something that sounds a little like "What cheer, cheer, cheer." Towhees sing, "Drink your tea." Ovenbirds sing, "Teacher, teacher, teacher." People have thought of these words to help them remember the songs. Most birds sing songs that are too complicated or too fast for words.

Which sentence below expresses the main idea?

A. Oven birds sing, "Teacher, teacher, teacher."

B. "Cardinals sing something that sounds a little like 'What cheer, cheer, cheer.'"

C. "Most birds sing songs that are too complicated or too fast for words."

D. "Each kind of bird has its own type of song."

4. When I watch my bird feeder, I often see different kinds of birds chasing each other. The feeder offers in one small place a large amount of food that many birds like and can get at easily. By scattering the seeds around on the ground, I can reduce the competition and the chasing.

This paragraph suggests that

A. birds are territorial.

B. birds sing to mark their territory.

C. there are different kinds of bird songs.

D. birds compete with one another for food.

5. Write a summary of this article. Include only the important ideas and details. Leave out unimportant ideas and details. Write your summary on a separate sheet of paper.

LA-C-E-5.9

There are three basic reasons, or purposes, for writing. An **author's purpose** for writing may be to:

Entertain Writing that **entertains** is for the reader's enjoyment. It may include personal narratives, humorous essays, books of jokes and puns, and true stories about strange and unusual events.

Inform Writing that **informs** includes a lot of facts and details about a topic. It includes newspaper and encyclopedia articles, books and articles about science and history, autobiographies and biographies.

Persuade Writing that **persuades** tries to convince the reader do something or to agree with the author's views. Usually, it contains opinions as well as facts. This type of writing includes editorials, campaign brochures, and advertisements.

The writer chooses what information to include and how to arrange it based on his or her purpose. Knowing the author's purpose will help you to choose an appropriate reading strategy.

Directions Read the selection below. Then answer the questions that follow it.

from **Nature's Blimps**
by Richard and Joyce Wolkomir

"A manatee is pulling my swim fin," biologist Bob Bonde tells us. He is snorkeling in Florida's Homosassa River. We are canoeing alongside. Peering down, we see an animal the size of a Volkswagon Beetle tugging with its flippers at one of Bonde's rubber swim fins.

"They're very curious," he shrugs.

A manatee would never hurt a minnow, much less a biologist. Weighing up to a ton or more, they have no natural enemies, not even this river's alligators. Also, they are vegetarians, peaceable grazers on sea plants, nicknamed "sea cows."

Their closest relatives are elephants. They do have gray, wrinkly elephant skin, although they squeak instead of trumpeting. The best description may be "giant gray sweet potatoes," which is what a ranger here at Homosassa Springs State Wildlife Park calls them.

Measuring Up® to the Ohio Academic Content Standards

Activity continued

Even so, manatees may have inspired the legend of mermaids. When Christopher Columbus first saw manatees, in 1493, he said, "These mermaids were not quite so handsome as they had been painted."

Manatees have blimpy bodies, giant beaver tails, and rubbery faces bristling with whiskers. They also have ridiculous-looking little flippers. But they can use their flippers almost like hands. They even have "fingernails," a holdover from the days when their ancestors had feet rather than flippers and walked on land. So a manatee can pick things up with its flippers, like a tasty clump of seagrass, and hold it just so. Or, like the manatee under our canoe, it can tug at a snorkeling biologist's swim fin. "They see anything new as a toy to investigate," he tells us.

We are hanging out with Bob Bonde, who studies manatees for the U.S. Geological Survey. He gathers information about manatees to help them, because Florida's ever-growing human population makes life difficult for these gentle creatures.

Manatees are all around our canoe—snoozing on the bottom, investigating park visitors' kayaks, swimming alongside snorkelers and scuba divers. Every few minutes, a manatee surfaces to breathe, "whoosh."

This morning the air is only 40 degrees. We are shivering in our canoe. But the river is so warm steam is rising from it. It is because of that warmth that manatees congregate here on cold days. "Springs here heat the river to 72 degrees," Bob Bonde tells us. Manatees swim up here from the Gulf of Mexico to get warm."

People like warmth, too, and millions have migrated from the snowy North to Florida. The coasts are lined with houses, docks, and marinas. Pollution and dredging kill the seagrass that manatees eat. Buzzing boats—Florida has about 830,000 registered boaters— frequently hit manatees. Some die. Others are scarred for life.

Activity continued

"Just about every Florida manatee has scars on its back where it was cut up by boat propellers," says Bonde. (Almost all of them have been hit more than once, and one manatee was struck 49 times before it was actually killed.) In fact scientists identify individual manatees by their scar patterns. Bonde is snorkeling in the Homosassa River to look for manatees with unfamiliar scars. When he spots one, he snaps its picture for the statewide manatee photo album. That way, scientists like him can follow individual manatees, learning how they spend their days, how they die, or how they survive.

1. Could you identify the author's purpose by only reading the title of the selection? Why or why not?

   _____

   _____

2. Read the paragraph below.

   A manatee would never hurt a minnow, much less a biologist. Weighing up to a ton or more, they have no natural enemies, not even this river's alligators. Also, they are vegetarians, peaceable grazers on sea plants, nicknamed "sea cows."

   What do you learn about manatees from reading this paragraph?

   _____

   _____

       Measuring Up® to the Ohio Academic Content Standar

Activity continued

3. Read the paragraph below.

> Manatees have blimpy bodies, giant beaver tails, and rubbery faces bristling with whiskers. They also have ridiculous-looking little flippers. But they can use their flippers almost like hands. They even have "fingernails," a holdover from the days when their ancestors had feet rather than flippers and walked on land. So a manatee can pick things up with its flippers, like a tasty clump of seagrass, and hold it just so. Or, like the manatee under out canoe, it can tug at a snorkeling biologist's swim fin. "They see anything new as a toy to investigate," he tells us.

What do you learn about a manatee's flippers from this paragraph?

_____

_____

_____

4. What do you think was the author's main purpose for writing this article?

_____

_____

_____

Understand Author's Purpose

Directions: Use the article you just read to answer questions 1–5.

1. Even so, manatees may have inspired the legend of mermaids. When Christopher Columbus first saw manatees, in 1493, he said, "These mermaids were not quite so handsome as they had been painted."

    The main purpose of this paragraph is to

    A. describe the events of 1493.

    B. tell why Christopher Columbus became an explorer.

    C. paint an unfavorable picture of manatees.

    D. explain the possible origin of the myth of mermaids.

2. The author included all of the details below to support the idea that manatee are gentle EXCEPT

    A. "A manatee is pulling my swim fin," biologist Bob Bonde tells us.

    B. A manatee would never hurt a minnow, much less a biologist.

    C. Their closest relatives are elephants.

    D. The best description may be "giant gray sweet potatoes," which is what a ranger here at Homosassa Springs State Wildlife Park calls them.

       Measuring Up® to the Ohio Academic Content Standards

3. What is the main reason why scientists study manatees in Florida?

    A. They are large, gentle vegetarians.

    B. The U.S. Geological Society studies the environment.

    C. There is not enough information about manatees.

    D. They are endangered.

4. From the information in the last paragraph, what does the reader learn about manatee?

    A. Manatees enjoy having their picture taken.

    B. Only one manatee has been actually killed by a boat propeller.

    C. Scientists identify manatees by their scars.

    D. It is difficult to track manatees.

5. Summarize what you learned about manatees from reading this article. Write your response on a separate sheet of paper.

Analyze Arguments and Persuasive Techniques

LA-C-D-5.9

An **argument** gives the author's **position** on an issue. An author uses this form of writing to **persuade** the reader to accept his or her suggestion/position.

This type of text structure is often used in

- editorials;
- book and movie reviews;
- advertisements;
- letters to the editor of the newspaper;
- political speeches.

When you read an argument, determine the author's **position**. What is the author calling for, or proposing, to be done? What is the proposition? Look for the main idea or point the author wants you to agree with or accept. As you read, think about whether the author is being fair. Is the author including misleading statements in an attempt to persuade readers?

Then look at the evidence that the author includes. Does the author use relevant facts and details to **support** the argument, or proposition? Or is the author including only evidence that stirs up your emotions and prevents you from thinking clearly?

Finally, evaluate the information and decide whether it is accurate. Then decide whether you agree with the author's position.

Activity

Directions Read the letter to the editor below. Then answer the questions that follow it.

1701 Mercer Avenue

Mentor, OH 44060

July 15

Dear Editor:

I am a teacher at Spencer Elementary School. On my way to school last Thursday, I walked past the empty lot on Forester Street. It was littered with discarded soda cans, old newspapers, and wrappers from people's meals. What an eyesore! Not only did it look bad, it smelled. In fact, the odor was so bad I had to cross to the other side of the street.

I have discussed this situation with my fellow teachers and we have a proposal. We feel so strongly that this proposal would benefit everyone that we are winning to dedicate our own time and services to make it work.

We propose that the town turn this empty lot into a community garden for kids. The lot is of no use to anyone right now. In fact, it is a hazard. Anyone walking through it could get hurt by the broken glass or shards of metal. The garbage can cause health problems. The smell, particularly on hot summer days, assaults the senses. Turning this lot into a community garden would quickly change a problem into an asset. Instead of a smelly, dirty lot, the town would gain a beautiful oasis.

Another benefit of this proposal is that it would be good for kids. It would give them a place to be outdoors in good weather. Kids would stay out of trouble since the garden would be supervised by teachers.

Kids would learn responsibility. They would each be assigned a specific patch in the garden. It would be their job to tend that patch. Within a short time, they would see the effects of their care or their lack of care. And the other kids working in the garden would see it, too.

Activity continued

In addition, working in the garden would teach kids about nature. We would teach the students about plants and their care and students would have first-hand experience working as gardeners. They would choose the plants to grow, plant the seeds, tend them, and watch what happens. They would learn the effects of weather condition on plants as well as the effects of too much or too little water.

The garden would be self-supporting. At first the teachers would support it with some help from parents. Eventually, students could sell the flowers and vegetables they grow to pay for seeds and other supplies.

In conclusion, this proposal has no drawbacks and many benefits. The town does not have to contribute anything but a dirty smelly lot. The town would gain an attractive space and its kids would have a place to be outdoors, learn responsibility, and discover facts about nature.

Sincerely yours,

Melanie Trevani

1. Why did the author write this letter? What does she want to persuade the town to do?

_____

_____

2. Why does the author mention the broken glass, the garbage, and the smell?

_____

_____

     Measuring Up® to the Ohio Academic Content Standar

Activity continued

3. Write the sentence from the third paragraph that tells what the town would gain by going along with the author's proposal.

     _____

     _____

4. According to the author, what three things would kids gain from the garden?

     _____

     _____

     _____

5. Did the author persuade you to agree with her position? Why or why not?

     _____

     _____

     _____

Apply to the Test

Directions: Use the selection you just read to answer questions 1–5.

1. The author would probably agree with which of the following statements?

    A. The town should not be concerned about the empty lot.

    B. The empty lot presents a serious problem to the town.

    C. The town should build an apartment building on the empty lot.

    D. The town should require teachers to improve the empty lot.

2. The author wrote this article mainly to

    A. entertain readers with an amusing story.

    B. describe an empty lot in town.

    C. inform readers about how to set up a garden.

    D. persuade readers to turn an empty lot into a community garden.

3. Which statement from the article best expresses what the author wants to persuade the town to do?

    A. "On my way to school last Thursday, I walked past the empty lot on Forester Street."

    B. "I have discussed this situation with my fellow teachers and we have a proposal."

    C. "We propose that the town turn this empty lot into a community garden for kids."

    D. "Another benefit of the proposal is that it would be good for kids."

4. Which detail below does NOT support the author's proposal?

    A. The empty lot smells bad and is an eyesore.

    B. The teacher walks past the empty lot on her way to school.

    C. Kids could learn about nature as they work in the garden.

    D. The garden would be self-supporting so the town wouldn't have to pay for it.

5. The author gave several reasons to support her proposal. Which reason do you think was the most effective? Tell why. Write your answer on a separate sheet of paper.

Draw Conclusions from Different Sources

LA-C-E-5.8, LA-C-F-5.3

When you read, you may have to **draw conclusions** about a text or a story. A **conclusion** is a judgment you form by adding up the evidence. You use logical reasoning to arrive at a new understanding. For example, suppose you read that a boy bends down to pet the dog. Then you read that the dog jumps up onto a little girl's lap and curls up. Next you read that the father carries the dog in a shoulder bag. By adding up the evidence, you logically conclude that the dog is small.

To draw conclusions, you should:

- Look for two or more facts or details the author provides about a character or event. These facts have to be relevant. If the information is relevant, or important, then it will support the conclusion.
- Based on these facts, use logical reasoning to draw a conclusion.
- Ask yourself whether the conclusion makes sense.
- As you continue reading, ask yourself whether the new information requires you to rethink your conclusion. If so, revise your conclusion.

Sometimes, you read more than one selection about the same topic. Then compare and contrast the information and the conclusions the writers make. Draw your own conclusions based on the evidence in both selections.

Look at the treatment, the scope, and the organization of both selections.

Treatment is the way the author handles the topic. For example, two writers may write about pollution. One writer deals with this subject in a straightforward, objective manner. She includes many facts and details in an informative article. Another writer treats this same subject in a more subjective way. He writes a personal essay. He includes emotion-filled letters from people affected by pollution.

Scope is the range of the information. For example, one writer focuses on only one of the events leading up to World War I. Another covers all of the major events.

Organization is the way the writer arranges the information. For example, one writer arranges the information in chronological order. He shows what event happened first, second, and so on. Another arranges the information in a cause-and-effect pattern. She shows the result of each action or decision.

Activity **Directions** Read the article below. Then answer the questions that follow it.

Hieroglyphics
from The Knowledge Factory
edited by Kate Gillett

The Ancient Egyptians spoke a language related to the languages of the Middle East and North Africa. Those who could, wrote using a system of picture writing called hieroglyphics. The Egyptians began using hieroglyphics in about 3000 B.C. This was shortly after the first known examples of writing appeared in Sumer (now southeastern Iraq). Each picture, or hieroglyph, could stand for an object and a sound. Some represented one letter, others up to five letters. These were always consonants. Vowels were not written down.

Breaking the Code

Hieroglyphics were last used in about A.D. 394. For more than 1,400 years, no one could read or understand them. In 1799, however, a soldier in Napoleon Bonaparte's army in Egypt found a large stone slab—the Rosetta Stone. On the stone was a text carved by Egyptian priests in 196 B.C. to mark the crowning of King Ptolemy V. The same text was written out in Ancient Egyptian hieroglyphs, demotic script (a simpler form of hieroglyphs), and Greek. By comparing the three, a French scholar called Jean-François Champollion was finally able to crack the code in 1822.

Writing Hieroglyphs

The word *hieroglyph* is Greek for sacred carvings. Egyptian hieroglyphs were usually written or carved by highly trained men called scribes. Egyptian society was based on keeping records. Scribes were therefore very important. Many rose to positions of great authority because they could read and write.

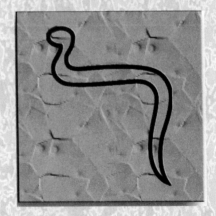

Activity continued

  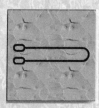   

Papyrus Paper

The Egyptians wrote on a paper-like material, called papyrus, made of reeds. The pith was taken out of the reeds and cut into strips. These were laid flat in layers, covered with cloth, and pounded with heavy stones or a mallet to weld them together.

The papyrus was then polished to give a smooth, flat surface. Sheets of papyrus were often put together to form a roll.

Hieroglyphs were not used in everyday life. They were reserved for important inscriptions, such as those on tombs and temples and for affairs of state.

For daily use, two simpler, less formal shorthand scripts were created. Hieratic script was used in the Old Kingdom. By about 700 B.C., demotic (from the Greek word *demotikos*, meaning "popular") script was in use.

There were many different ways of writing hieroglyphs. They could be written from left to right, right to left or top to bottom. If an animal faced right, you read from right to left. If it faced left, you read from left to right.

The name or symbol of a ruler appeared in hieroglyphs within an oval frame called a cartouche.

Champollion solved the puzzle of the Rosetta Stone using names like Ptolemy and Cleopatra.

Activity continued

1. What is the topic of this article?

     _____

2. How does the writer treat this topic?

     _____

     _____

3. The writer organizes the information into several categories. Which
    paragraph tells you mostly about what group of people used
    hieroglyphics and when they used them? Under what heading do you
    find information about the scribes who kept records using hieroglyphics?

     _____

     _____

4. Read the paragraph below.

     The Egyptians wrote on a paper-like material, called papyrus,
     made of reeds. The pith was taken out of the reeds and cut into
     strips. These were laid flat in layers, covered with cloth, and pounded
     with heavy stones or a mallet to weld them together.

     What detail in this paragraph might lead you to conclude the reeds were
     plentiful in ancient Egypt?

     _____

     _____

5. What details in this article might lead you to conclude that writing
    hieroglyphics was difficult?

     _____

     _____

Apply to the Test

Directions: Use both of the articles you just read to answer questions 1–5.

1. All of the information below can be found only in "Seeker of Knowledge" EXCEPT

   A. personal details of Champollion's life.

   B. Champollion's thoughts and words.

   C. how Champollion deciphered hieroglyphics.

   D. what Champollion did after he deciphered hieroglyphics.

2. All of the details below describe "Hieroglyphics" EXCEPT

   A. very personal or subjective style.

   B. information organized in categories.

   C. purpose is mainly to inform.

   D. contains many facts and details.

3. You could use this article to draw conclusions about

   A. a soldier in 1799.

   B. methods used to decipher codes.

   C. keeping records in ancient Egypt.

   D. how papyrus is made.

4. Which statement below does NOT describe "Hieroglyphics"?

   A. contains literary descriptions

   B. provides an explanation of hieroglyphics

   C. discusses the Rosetta Stone

   D. contains information about Napoleon

5. Draw a conclusion about life in Ancient Egypt. Use a fact or detail from each article to support your conclusion. That means you need to provide two facts or details. Write your answer on a separate sheet of paper.

LA-C-A-5.1, LA-C-A-5.5, LA-C-A-5.6, LA-C-B-5.2, LA-C-B-5.7,
LA-C-C-5.4, LA-C-D-5.9, LA-C-E-5.8, LA-C-E-5.9, LA-C-F-5.3

Directions: Read the selection.

Summer Camp Hawaiian Style
by Cynthia Berger

Would you dare climb an active volcano? Twelve-year-old Branden Kekauli's Kahawai did.

Brandon hiked up Mount Kilauea on the Big Island of Hawaii as part of a summer program called *Na Pua No-eau*. This Hawaiian-language name means "Flower of Wisdom." *Na Pua* teaches native Hawaiian kids how their ancestors lived—and how this wisdom can be part of their lives today.

In one *Na Pua* program, for example, kids learn to sail a traditional Hawaiian canoe. They navigate the modern way, with instruments and charts. But they also learn to find their way as their ancestors did—by natural guideposts, such as stars and ocean currents. And sailing the big canoe requires the Hawaiian value of *laulima*—working together.

Rocking and Rolling

The volcano program is called "Rocks and Rolls." Branden and other kids hiked across fields of jagged lava in Hawaii Volcanoes National Park. They learned all about volcanoes in two very different ways.

From one *kuma* (teacher), a scientist from the United States Geological Survey, the kids learned to identify the different kinds of volcanic rock, and all about volcanic eruptions.

From another *kuma*, who is a native Hawaiian, the kids learned what Hawaiians of long ago thought about volcanoes.

They learned that you should behave respectfully when visiting *wahi pana*—places on the volcano that are sacred to Hawaiians. No shouting or throwing stones! And the kids learned ancient *mo'olelo* (stories) and songs about volcanoes. They learned how to do a volcano dance. The movements imitate the way lava (molten rock) crackles and crunches as it slowly flows along.

Health and Medicine, Too

At school, Kaimanu Pine is trying out for the wrestling team. During the *Nā Pua* summer program about health and medicine, he found himself flat on a mat—but not for wrestling. "We learned how to do traditional Hawaiian massage therapy," Kaimanu explains. "Our *kumu* gave me a massage to show the other kids how it's done."

The kids in Kaimanu's class also learned how to get oil from the nuts of the kukui tree. (This oil smoothes the skin during traditional massage.) The kids roasted nuts over a campfire, then ground the nuts in an old-fashioned mortar and pestle made of stone. Oil oozed out of the mashed nuts.

Other days, Kaimanu and his friends went for hikes in the forest. Their *kumu*, Aunty Alapa's Kahuena, taught them how to recognize native plants that can be used as medicines. "I teach the children to be respectful when taking things from the land," says Aunty Kahuena. "Before you pick, you should ask the plant's permission, and explain what it will be used for. And afterwards, you should say 'thank you.'"

Kaimanu also discovered that modern science and ancient wisdom can agree. "According to traditional Hawaiian medicine, juice from *noni* (a native fruit) is good for your immune system," says Kaimanu. "Nowadays, doctors think *noni* might be a treatment for cancer."

The First Hawaiians

Hawaiians of long ago were a lot like modern scientists. They made careful observations of the natural world; then they tried to come up with reasonable explanations of unusual events, such as storms or volcanic eruptions.

But just who were the ancestors of today's Hawaiian kids? The first people came to Hawaii about fifteen hundred years ago. They traveled across the Pacific Ocean from Polynesia in sailing canoes, bring coconut trees and other plants, as well as dogs and pugs.

As fishermen and farmers, the people tried to live in harmony with the land. They had their own laws, language, and religion. They lived in little villages and were ruled by local chiefs.

In recent times the old ways of Hawaii were almost lost. "Through *Nā Pua No'eau*, kids discover that we can learn from our past," says Terry Reveira, a *kumu* and native Hawaiian. "We can use what we learn to plan our future."

Reaching for the Stars

Whether they are studying volcanoes or sailing, all kids in *Nā Pua No'eau* learn hula (dancing) and *kukulu kumuhana* (Hawaiian chants). Some of the dances and chants tell stories about famous Hawaiians of long ago. Others describe special places on the islands.

On the last day of camp, the kids put on a show. Everyone wears a flower *lei* (necklace). "We share what we learned with our families," says Kaimanu.

Nā Pua No'eau helps kids to feel proud of the past. And it helps them to reach for the stars in the future. "I always was interested in volcanoes," says Branden. "But I never thought about being a scientist who studies them." Now he says, "I'm thinking I could be a scientist when I grow up."

History of Hawaii

About A.D. 500	First people come to Hawaii.
Late 1700s	Europeans come to Hawaii.
Early 1800s	Hawaii becomes an independent nation under King Kamehameha the Great.
Late 1800s–1900	Queen Liliuokalani is dethroned; Hawaii becomes an American territory.
1959	Hawaii becomes the 50th U.S. state.

Directions: Use the selection to answer questions 1-10.

1. They learned all about volcanoes in two very different ways.

    This sentence suggests that the rest of the information in this section will be organized in what way?

    A. by cause and effect

    B. by chronological order

    C. by comparison and contrast

    D. by classification

2. Which statement from this article is an example of an opinion?

    A. "But I never thought about being a scientist who studies them."

    B. "They learned that you should behave respectfully when visiting *wahi pana*—places on the volcano that are sacred to Hawaiians."

    C. "Before you pick, you should ask the plant's permission, and explain what it will be used for."

    D. "They traveled across the Pacific Ocean from Polynesia in sailing canoes, bring coconut trees and other plants, as well as dogs and pugs."

3. Noni might be effective as a treatment for cancer because

    A. it is an ancient Hawaiian remedy.

    B. its juice boosters the immune system.

    C. the noni is a native fruit of Hawaii.

    D. people have used it for many years.

4. Which statement below BEST supports the idea that the ancient Hawaiians understood how to use plants as medicines?

    A. "Nowadays, doctors think noni might be a treatment for cancer."

    B. "Before you pick, you should ask the plant's permission, and explain what it will be used for."

    C. "Other days, Kaimanu and his friends went for hikes in the forest."

    D. "Their *kumu*, Aunty Alapa's Kahuena, taught them how to recognize native plants that can be used as medicines."

5. Explain the author's purpose for writing this article. Be sure to include three details from the article to support your response. Write your response on a separate sheet of paper.

6. The information under the heading "The First Hawaiians" is provided to

    A. inform.

    B. show cause and effect.

    C. entertain.

    D. persuade.

7. Which statement below BEST explains why native Hawaiians feel it is important to study the past?

    A. "In recent times the old ways of Hawaii were almost lost."

    B. "The first people came to Hawaii about fifteen hundred years ago."

    C. "Na Pua No'eau helps kids to feel proud of the past."

    D. "We can use what we learn to plan our future."

8. How is *Na Pua No'eau* MOST like other ceremonies throughout the world?

    A. It teaches the importance of massage therapy.

    B. It shows kids how to climb volcanoes.

    C. It teaches young people how to sail in traditional canoes.

    D. It helps young people connect with their heritage.

9. Look at the map. In what direction would you travel if you went from Honolulu to Kauai?

    A. northeast

    B. northwest

    C. southeast

    D. southwest

10. Did Branden enjoy his experience at summer camp? Tell whether he did or did not. Use at least three details from the article to support your response. Then tell whether you would enjoy a similar experience. Write your response on a separate sheet of paper.

Acknowledgments

p. 5, "Keeping Cool with Crickets" by Lois Jacobson, originally published in *Cricket* Magazine, August 1992, and *Spider* Magazine, June 2003, Copyright © 2004 by Lois Jacobson. Reprinted by permission of the author; p. 10, "How Do Owls Hunt at Night?" by Edna Manning. Reprinted by permission of CRICKET magazine, December 2002, Vol. 30, No. 4, Copyright © 2002 by Carus Publishing Company; p. 17, "Fabulous Frederic" Reprinted by permission of SPIDER magazine, March 2005, Vol. 12, No. 3, Copyright © 2005 by Peggy Thorne; p. 25, excerpt from "Small Dog Blues" Reprinted by permission of CRICKET magazine, March 1998, Vol. 25, No. 7, Copyright © 1998 by Bonnie Brightman; p. 32, excerpt from "The Clarinet" Reprinted by permission of CRICKET magazine, August 1997, Vol. 24, No. 12, Copyright © 1997 by Glenn Dixon; p. 39, "E is for Encyclopedia" from ABECEDARIAN by Charles W. Ferguson. Copyright © 1964 by Charles W. Ferguson. By permission of Little, Brown and Company, Inc.; p. 44, "Superheroes and Mischievous Imps" by Randall Lewis; p. 51, "Smile! It's Sarah Bear" by Charline Profiri, Copyright © 2004 by Highlights for Children, Inc., Columbus, Ohio; p. 58, "Inca Treasure in the Cloud Forest" by Peter Lourie, Copyright © 1990 by Highlights for Children, Inc., Columbus, Ohio; p. 69, "The Wag-o-meter Study" Reprinted by permission of SPIDER magazine, October 1999, Vol. 6, No. 10, Copyright © 1999 by Suzanne M. Baur; p. 73, "It's a Squawker! by Andy Boyles, Copyright © 2002 by Highlights for Children, Inc., Columbus, Ohio; p. 76, "Your Amazing Body Clock" by Karen K. McCoy, from Children's Digest, copyright © 2000 by Children's Better Health Institute, Benjamin Franklin Literary & Medical Society, Indianapolis, Indiana. Used by permission; p. 82, "The Ghost of Yuckachi Swamp" by Crystal Mandell, copyright © 2003 by Highlights for Children, Inc., Columbus, Ohio; p. 86, "No More, No Less" Reprinted by permission of SPIDER magazine, January 2005, Vol. 12, No. 1, Copyright © 2004 by Marci Stillerman; p. 92, "Bodacious Bode Miller" by Molly Lowry; p. 99, "Tree of Plenty" Reprinted by permission of CRICKET magazine, December 2001, Vol. 29, No. 4, Copyright © 2001 by Bo Flood; p. 108, excerpt from "Those Three Bears" by Ruskin Bond, Copyright © 2004 by Highlights for Children, Inc., Columbus, Ohio; p. 115, "Bird's Nest Soup" by Barabara D. Lopossa, from Children's Digest Magazine, December 2000. Copyright © 2000 by Children's Better Health Institute, Benjamin Franklin Literary & Medical Society, Indianapolis, Indiana; p. 125, "The Hummingbird Trail" by Jennifer Owings Dewey, Copyright © 2002 by Highlights for Children, Inc., Columbus; p. 131, "Bodies in Motion" by Edith H. Fine and Judith P. Josephson, from Children's Digest, copyright © 1991 by Children's Better Health Institute, Benjamin Franklin Literary & Medical Society, Inc., Indianapolis, Indiana. Used by permission; p. 141, "The Great Bunk Bed War" Reprinted by permission of SPIDER magazine, November 2002, Vol. 9, No. 11, Copyright © 2002 by Lisa Harkrader; p. 145, "My Korean Name" by Leonard Chang, Copyright © 1999 by Highlights for Children, Inc. Columbus, Ohio; p. 153, "Run to the River" by Pamela Kuck, Copyright © 1998 by Highlights for Children, Inc., Columbus, Ohio; p. 160, "Coasting Free" Reprinted by permission of CRICKET magazine, December 1996, Vol. 24, No. 4, Copyright © 1996 by Janet Plumb Jones; p. 168, "Swimming Lesson" by John Moir, Copyright © 1998 by Highlights for Children, Inc., Columbus, Ohio; p. 176, "Will Power" by Kimberly Brubaker Bradley, Copyright © 1999 by Highlights for Children, Inc., Columbus, Ohio; p. 186, "Wilma Rudolph" by Judith P. Josephson, from *Children's Digest*, copyright © 1995 by Children's Better Health Institute, Benjamin Franklin Literary & Medical Society, Inc., Indianapolis, Indiana. Used by permission; p. 188, Getty Images; p. 194, "The Bogeys of Old Lucky Mine" Reprinted by permission of SPIDER magazine, October 2002, Vol. 9, No. 10, Copyright © 2002 by Joann Mazzio; p. 202, "Riding the Whale" by Liz Gallagher, Copyright © 2004 by Highlights for Children, Inc., Columbus, Ohio; p. 209, "Señor Coyote and the Tricked Trickster" retold by Linda K. Garrity, Used with permission from Talespinner: Folktales, Themes, and Activities retold by Linda Garrity, © 1999, Fulcrum Publishing, Inc., Golden, Colorado. All rights reserved; p. 221, "Sandra on Sports" by Sandra Neil, Copyright © 2000 by Highlights for Children, Inc., Columbus, Ohio; p. 224, photograph, by Sandra Neil; p. 227, "The Man Who Painted Truth" by Kathleen M. Hayes, Copyright © 2003 by Highlights for Children, Inc. Columbus, Ohio; p. 227, "Oscar Howe, CREATION OF WEONTANICA," 1975, casein on paper, 18 7/8" h x 28" w. Collection of the University of South Dakota. Copyright, University of South Dakota, 1975; p. 234, "United Nations" from *The World Almanac for Kids 2004*. Copyright © 2005 World Almanac Education Group. All Rights Reserved; p. 249, "Stop That Airliner" by Peter Price, published by Boys' Quest Magazine, August/September 2001. Reprinted by permission; p. 249, photos.com; p. 255, "Reaching for the Sky" by Kim Williams, Copyright © 1997 by Highlights for Children, Inc., Columbus, Ohio; p. 263, "Why Do Birds Sing?" by Mary Sue Waser, Copyright © 1990 by Highlights for Children, Inc., Columbus, Ohio; p. 263, photos.com; p. 270, excerpt from "Nature's Blimps" by Richard and Joyce Wolkomir, published in MUSE magazine, September 2002, Vol. 6, No. 7, Copyright © 2002 by Richard and Joyce Wolkomir. Reprinted by permission of the authors; p. 282, "Hieroglyphics" from The Knowledge Factory, Edited by Kate Gillett, Copyright © 1996 by Aladdin Books Ltd. Reprinted by permission of Aladdin Books Ltd.; p. 287, "Summer Camp Hawaiian Style" by Cynthia Berger, Copyright © 2004 by Highlights for Children, Inc., Columbus, Ohio; p. 287, photos.com

     Measuring Up® to the Ohio Academic Content Standa

Graphic Organizer
Sequencing Chart

First

Second

Third

After That

Finally

Main Idea

Important Detail

Important Detail

Important Detail

Important Detail

Important Detail

Conclusion